Newcast

City Council

Newcastle Libraries and Information Service

☎ **0845 002 0336**

2/08

Due for return	Due for return	Due for return
−5 MAR 2008 5|11		
29 APR 2008		
−3 OCT 2008		
1 0 JUN 2009		
−7 JAN 2010		
2 6 AUG 2010		

Please return this item to any of Newcastle's Libraries by the last
date shown above. If not requested by another customer the loan
can be renewed, you can do this by phone, post or in person.
Charges may be made for late returns.

LEWIS HAMILTON
THE STORY SO FAR

GARETH ROGERS

Cover illustrations © PA Photos
Plates 2-12 also © PA Photos

First published 2007

STADIA is an imprint of
Tempus Publishing
Cirencester Road, Chalford
Stroud, Gloucestershire, GL6 8PE
www.tempus-publishing.com

© Gareth Rogers, 2007

The right of Gareth Rogers to be identified as the Author
of this work has been asserted in accordance with the
Copyrights, Designs and Patents Act 1988.

British Library Cataloguing in Publication Data.
A catalogue record for this book is available from the British Library.

ISBN 978 07524 4480 2

Typesetting and origination by NPI Media Group
Printed in Great Britain

CONTENTS

Chapter One

FAST IMPRESSIONS

There is the glamour of the Formula One circuit and there is the Rye House Kart Track. It sits next to the Rye House Speedway Stadium, over the bridge from the local railway station, and is overshadowed by a Sainsbury's distribution centre. Yet it is here that Lewis Hamilton's racing career began.

Martin Hines is the proprietor of the kart manufacturing company Zipkart based on site and he recalls: 'I was with one of my young guns – Anthony Davidson or Gary Paffret – keeping an eye on the cadet race for eight to ten year olds.

'Novices usually wear black plates for their first six races and they normally congregate at the back of the field. But I noticed one up in the top four and thought it was unusual and it must be the last of his six races.'

Martin was obviously curious to find out who this young boy was and introduced himself to his father, Anthony. Then came the revelation that this was their first race meeting. Impressed, an invitation was made by Martin to come and chat about the future. 'Money was obviously not that plentiful and I thought I could help out. That chat started a relationship that lasted eight years.'

Someone off the street would not have noticed the black number plate but for Martin Hines this was somebody who was special. The next day he offered to supply little Lewis with a kart chassis. In return he found a youngster who was intelligent, willing to learn and talented. 'An exceptional kid from an exceptional family.'

Lewis himself remembers two aspects of those early days in a kart. First, that helmet colour, chosen so Anthony could spot young Lewis: 'Dad wanted me to have a bright-coloured helmet because he was so nervous when I was on track.' Then the hidden risks: 'I don't think my parents knew how dangerous it could be. I had one big crash, bashed my head and had a nosebleed, but just told Dad to fix the kart. The next day I raced and won.'

The Hamilton family also competed at Buckmore Park near Chatham in Kent. Bill Sisley, the Buckmore Park chairman, recalls: 'Lewis had been coming here with his father since he was eight. You could see straightaway that he had something. Because the Cadets are so basic it is much more about the driver than the machine. Within two or three laps I can see if a boy is different. They have a touch and a talent that sets them apart. What you are looking for is natural speed allied to competitive edge, and the intelligence to react to changing circumstances.

'Lewis always had terrific natural speed. We are talking about a feel and a balance of the car underneath him. He is a great overtaker, takes a great line through a course and above all he wants to win.'

By 1996, when Lewis was eleven, Martin Hines and Ron Dennis of McLaren had set up the McLaren Mercedes Champions of the Future series – an ITV networked programme. 'The aim was to showcase the talent in karting. The ironic thing was that in the first year, 1996, Lewis Hamilton was champion in the cadet formula and Gary Paffret was champion in the top Intercontinental A category. Ten years later, these two were fighting it out to win the 2007 McLaren drive alongside Fernando Alonso.'

At the final event in October 1996 young Lewis was on pole position for his first British Championship final with a national TV audience, and in the presence of Mika Häkkinen, Martin Brundle, Mark Blundell and one Ron Dennis. Says Martin: 'The pressure was phenomenal and he handled it stunningly. That's why he started his Formula One career so well. He's lived with that kind of pressure.'

What of Ron Dennis? The duo first met at an awards ceremony in London in 1995 when the ten-year-old Hamilton made an immediate impact on the McLaren supremo: 'When I first met Lewis he was asking for my autograph. Unlike so many people, he looked me square in the face and informed me where he was going in his life. Without breaking eye contact, he told me how he was going to go about his career. It impressed the hell out of me.' A couple of years later Ron Dennis was to sign Lewis Hamilton up to the McLaren development programme.

Before that, Lewis had caught the attention of Tony Purnell, the former boss of Jaguar Racing and now the FIA's technical director: 'I first came across him at a bleak kart track during testing. I asked who the kid in the yellow helmet was, because, watching from trackside, he looked pretty useful to me. I think he was then nine years old. Funnily enough, I only remember people saying how good he was, not that he was black, his other point of difference. When he was eleven or twelve, I remember chatting to him and his Dad on top of a steep bank at Wigan. What I remember is how he rode his bike. He had the elegance of an acrobat, slowly and effortlessly gliding down this very steep slope. Chatting to a friend as he did so, unaware that there was anything particularly remarkable about what he was doing. He had the ability to balance motionlessly on his bike at a dead stop and I remember thinking that grace and balance of that order are qualities that go hand in hand with being a very good racing driver.'

After that, Tony arranged for his company, Pi Research, to start sponsoring Lewis. Soon he grew friendly with the Hamilton family and recalls that he found them a total joy to deal with. Every year Tony would receive a framed photograph of Lewis in action and one year he received a set of crystal glasses to let him know they really appreciated the support.

At twelve Lewis managed to acquire that most important of all assets for an aspiring race driver – a worthy 'Godfather' in the shape of McLaren's Ron Dennis. Says Tony Purnell:

'Ron owned the competitor – Tag Electronics – to my company Pi Research. But I rolled over happily because I appreciated that Ron was absolutely the best backer that Lewis could have wished for. And Ron backed Lewis big time, getting him the best seats and best support a driver could have.'

John Seal was Lewis's headmaster at junior school in Stevenage: 'He stood out at school and not just because he was winning all those karting trophies. He was popular, he was composed when it came to speaking in public, and he was focused, exceptionally for one so young. More than anything, I remember just how much support he got from his father. They were just an ordinary family from a hard-working background. That's why it's so good to see that things have turned out the way they have.'

A schoolmate at the John Henry Newman School in Stevenage was Aston Villa striker Ashley Young: 'I've seen that he's doing well and I'm happy for him. We used to talk about our ambitions at school, but as soon as we left we drifted apart. Because of his racing it was a bit difficult to be friends as he was in three days and then off and after a while I rarely saw him. He would be away at weekends so you couldn't really socialise out of school.'

However, they were members of the school football and cricket teams. 'He played centre midfield. He wasn't too bad, but I was a better player: that's why he's doing his driving. We played cricket as well. We were the worst ones on the team. I think we were just making the numbers up.'

Another friend that Lewis made was Luke Hines, son of Zipkart's Martin: 'As a kart driver he was brilliant. As a bloke, he was great fun. We'd go to under-18 discos, that kind of stuff. He was just like the rest of us – an ordinary young guy who liked to have a good time.'

On the more serious front, Tony Purnell reminds us of one interesting factor which flavoured his debut season in Formula One: 'It helps to note that Lewis has always comprehensively blown away his teammate. To emphasise the point, consider his teammate in Formula A [the top karting class], one Nico Rosberg. Significantly, both Nico and Lewis were racing for a team set up by Keke, Nico's ex-World Champion father.

'The boy who had been doing the over-performing had been doing it despite the real pressure of delivering in a team that the mega-competitive Keke had built! Taking on Alonso at McLaren would be no harder than that.'

So what was the career path that took Lewis to the pinnacle of the sport? As stated he was a McLaren Mercedes Champion of the Future in 1996, as well as securing the Sky TV Kart Masters title. In 1997 he moved up from the Cadet level to the Junior Yamaha class and, once again, immediately took the laurels, repeating his British title success from Cadets and taking the McLaren Mercedes Champion of the Future crown in the class.

Lewis took the Champion of the Future tag in 1998 and continued to progress through the karting ranks. He took runner-up honours in the 1999 JICA Championship to go with his Italian 'Industrialists' title and fourth place in the Italian national JICA series.

Paired in that 'dream team' with future FI rival Nico Rosberg, young Hamilton went one better the following year, his first full season in senior competition, whitewashing his opponents to take the four-round 2000 European FA title. That success led to the world title later in the year, before ending the decade with victory in the Masters event at Bercy. The successful campaign also led to Lewis being made a founder member of the BRDC 'Rising Star' scheme.

Having become the very best in karts, the young man from Hertfordshire began the move into cars. He achieved fifth overall in the 2001 Formula Renault winter series. The decision to skip Formula Ford and head straight for the winged categories was justified when he took third overall in the 2002 Formula Renault UK Championship. He collected three wins, three pole positions and three fastest laps en route. Lewis also raced in four of the nine Eurocup rounds, with Manor Motorsport, claiming fifth overall with some exciting runs.

Although the temptation to move up to F3 was great, Hamilton took the advice to remain in Formula Renault in 2003. It proved to be a wise move, with ten wins, eleven poles and nine fastest laps seeing him secure the UK title. Having gained the crown with two rounds left, Lewis finally made the move to F3. A tentative debut at Brands Hatch was curtailed by an accident that put him in hospital with concussion. He proved his resilience, however, by taking pole for the end-of-season Korean Superprix before another incident prevented victory.

A full-time F3 campaign was announced for 2004 but not in the British Championship, rather the F3 Euroseries. Lewis enjoyed a solid debut year, taking one win and two thirds to end the season fifth in the standings. Then he dominated the inaugural Bahrain Superprix and took race one at Macau, the event being eventually won by future GP2 teammate Alex Premat.

Adopting the same strategy as in Formula Renault, young Hamilton did the same again in 2005 but left Manor to join the crack ASM team in the Euroseries. The Briton blitzed his opposition, taking win after win to easily take the title with 15 victories, 13 poles and 15 fastest laps emphasising the dominance. His rise was also illustrated in the Blue Riband F3 events as he won the Marlboro Masters at Zandvoort, the Monaco Grand Prix support races and the Pau Grand Prix.

Those associated with his rise obviously have clear memories of their time with him. John Booth, as team boss of Manor Motorsport, took the karting champion into Formula Renault: 'McLaren asked us to give Lewis a test in our Formula Renault and tell them what we thought. We took him to a general test day at Mallory Park. He'd never driven a car before, not even a road car – and he crashed our Renault after three laps! But the boys put it back together again, and he went back out and went very quickly. It hadn't fazed him in the slightest.' Once on the team, John recalls: 'There were a few mistakes – what you'd expect from a seventeen-year-old – and he felt the pressure in '03 when he was the clear favourite. The early races didn't go to plan, but then, at Silverstone, he was running fifth when it started to rain, and on slicks in the wet he came through and won the race easily. As soon as his confidence was up that was it – he was hardly beaten for the rest of the year and won the title.

'Lewis ran with us in the F3 Euroseries in '04. We knew we had the best driver and thought we had the best car, but we were kidding ourselves. It was difficult because Lewis didn't have a competitive teammate who could have helped to pinpoint the problems, but he got a win at the Norisring and then we won the Bahrain Super Prix from the back of the grid. That was something special.'

In his second year in the ultra-competitive Formula Three series the ASM team co-owner Feredric Vasseur found Lewis's record of 15 race wins and the title 'breathtaking': 'I think he learned a lot in 2005 with ASM, and we learned a lot from him – and the same was true when he stepped up to GP2 in 2006 with ASM's sister team, ART Grand Prix. I feel he improved as a driver in his time with us. He had a great relationship with the team and all the guys were sure that he would do the right thing at the right time. We were very comfortable on the pit wall about him overtaking or pushing in qualifying. I think you can see that now with McLaren, even though he's a rookie in F1 terms. There is a lot of maturity there already. One important quality of Lewis's was that he would always say, if necessary, "I made a mistake". That is so important, because if you have a bad session, you always think about what you'll change on the car, and then maybe you'll go off in a wrong direction. Lewis is very honest. What that really shows is that he's totally confident in himself, and that makes a difference.'

There was now only one more category to conquer before Formula One but would the GP2 series be too tough to crack? While that was being pondered, Ron Dennis assured him that one day he would get a chance at the highest level: 'He will be in Formula One, there's no question of that. Many people ask if there is a possibility of him driving for McLaren next season. Well, it's not impossible but it's just one of the options. We've mapped out his year, he's going to concentrate on GP2 and we're not going to get distracted from that. As and when I feel it is appropriate, we'll give him the opportunity to test and really settle in to driving a Formula One car. Then, according to how that works out, we'll decide together the next best step.'

Added McLaren managing director Martin Whitmarsh: 'We believe he will be a McLaren driver in the future. We want to give him a sporting challenge, and we think he is good enough to consistently win in GP2. Once he has won that championship we can do some F1 testing and then if there is a good opportunity to go F1 racing in 2007 we would look at it seriously.

'We have paid his entire budget for the last eight or nine years and put a lot of time and effort in with Lewis. We wouldn't have been doing that unless we thought he will one day win a World Championship in a McLaren.'

Among the fastest in almost every winter test he attended, Lewis was signed to replace Rosberg alongside Premat in ASM's sister team ART Grand Prix. He was listed amid the pre-season favourites, despite his rookie status.

After a maiden podium at Valencia, the young Briton soon played himself into the series. There was a rare double win in round three at the Nurburgring after which he went on to add three more victories – at Monaco and twice at Silverstone following a three-abreast passing move at Becketts. Although he failed to take another chequered flag and faced stiff opposition from Nelson Piquet Junior, a series of consistent podium finishes meant Lewis finished 2006 with 114 points, twelve more than his Brazilian rival.

ART co-owner Nicolas Todt adds his perspective: 'During 2006, I got to know Lewis better and was always impressed by his attitude, commitment and ambition. He kept his feet on the ground, knowing it wouldn't be easy to beat Nelson Piquet Junior and become champion. We didn't only have good times in terms of performance, but he was never worried. Even if we were well down the order in practice, Lewis always took it calmly. He had such self-confidence and such belief in the team that it was a great motivation for everyone.'

There was speculation that he might make the step up to F1 towards the end of the year but his mentor Ron Dennis opted for caution and stuck with the Kimi Räikkönen–Pedro de la Rosa pairing formed when Juan Pablo Montoya was shown the door after the US Grand Prix.

However, his boss was to state: 'Lewis has an exceptional talent and his overall performance during the season gives you a definite sense of pride and satisfaction. The manner of his many outstanding performances this season, such as those at Silverstone and Turkey, has been phenomenal and he is a deserving champion.'

So Lewis was given a chance and impressed during his first two-day test. As speculation grew that he could partner the incoming Fernando Alonso at the team in 2007, one senior British Grand Prix driver voiced caution. David Coulthard, with over 200 races in a thirteen-year career, believed that Hamilton needed time to grow into the sport. 'He's got the talent and backing, so he should take the time to really grow and mature as a man,' said the Scot. 'I would advise him not to rush in, because if it doesn't work out then his could be a very short career. In terms of driving talent I think he's ready, but it's not just about whether you can drive the car or not,' added David. 'It's about how you handle the rollercoaster that is the life of a Formula One driver. Inevitably as a young man he's still probably living at home. He probably hasn't grown into living his own life off the track. If you imagine ten years from now, he will be a different man than he is today. It's really a question of how he manages the transition which determines whether he has the same success on the race track.'

Chapter Two

ONWARD AND UPWARD

Fernando Alonso had been confirmed very early for the 2007 season but there was speculation surrounding Lewis Hamilton, Pedro de la Rosa, Gary Paffret and even former McLaren World Champion Mika Häkkinen. Lewis Hamilton's position was made public in November 2006 with Pedro de la Rosa reverting to test driver.

The decision to appoint Lewis was made after Monza in late September and kept secret. Only his father and brother knew. The decision was relayed to the aspiring driver in Ron Dennis's sitting room. 'I was overwhelmed. It was a surreal feeling. I was sat on a couch opposite Ron at his home. He told me that McLaren had decided to take me as their new driver. It didn't kick in. I put on a professional face. I could see Ron was excited. He said I should be, too. Inside I was but it had been such a long wait. It was a warm feeling knowing the seat was mine.'

A lethal mix of drive, an exhaustive work ethic and a finely honed talent had taken Lewis to Formula One and his perspective that: 'I was always more ambitious than the other guys as I was growing up. I know I will be the best one day and I'm pretty sure that I'll be World Champion. I have thought that way since I was six.' The spectacular duels between McLaren aces Alain Prost and Ayrton Senna fired the imagination of a very young Lewis: 'I followed their fights and resolved to become World Champion one day.' Dennis later confirmed that Lewis had been a model pupil: 'Confidence is often coupled with arrogance, but there isn't an ounce of arrogance in Lewis. He listened, which so frequently young people don't, and progressively built his career. He's deserved this opportunity.'

Stories about the protégé had often focused on the driver's ethnicity – his grandfather came to Britain from Grenada in the 1950s – but the McLaren principal insisted this had never been a consideration for him. 'To be honest, it just doesn't register and never has. We're very aware of the ability of Lewis' colour to be used as a headline. But for us, it's just immaterial. We don't hide from the fact that he's from a mixed-race background, but it just doesn't matter. The Tiger Woods label makes you smile and you could argue it's a compliment, but it's just not relevant to our objectives. He's in the team because he's earned it and not because of his colour.'

As for Lewis's perspective: 'The only time I think about colour is when other people raise the issue. It has been my dream to drive in F1 since I saw Ayrton Senna in a McLaren when I was six years old. F1 is growing. I hope my involvement will encourage other ethnic groups to get involved. People will see from me that it is possible. I'm proud of who I am and where I came from. When I was growing up it was difficult to find someone in this sport to relate to. There will be a lot more people able to relate to me. Being the first black man in F1 doesn't matter to me, personally, but for the sport itself it probably means quite a lot.'

Lewis would not only have to contend with the label of the 'Tiger Woods of F1' but also the prospect of being in equal equipment to the best driver in the sport. Yet the Stevenage lad was obviously relishing working with Alonso: 'I view it as a positive, I think I can benefit from having such a strong teammate and I'm looking forward to working with him. I'm going to try and do the best job I can and learn from him as quickly as possible and eventually compete against him.'

Lewis was wisely avoiding talk of victories, with Ron Dennis stating that having such a strong driver already in the team would actually give the newcomer space to develop. Yet at that early stage he thought the youngster could win a race in the forthcoming season: 'Having an expectation of Lewis winning next season is not unrealistic, as long as we have a strong car, but certainly not in the early parts of the season.' Time would tell! Dennis continued, 'One of his greatest qualities is his ability never to give up. That is the spirit I expect to see, no matter where he qualifies or where he finishes.'

It was the Christmas spirit rather than a fighting spirit that also presented Lewis in an interesting light. Sir Jackie

Stewart is president of the Springfield Club in Hackney. Each festive season he would present a sporting star to the youth section – most of whom were living in deprived circumstances on tough housing estates. For Christmas 2006 he booked the new kid on the F1 block. Reported the three-times World Champion of Lewis Hamilton: 'He was magic. It was mostly one-parent families, mostly black, a very mixed group and he was just the best guest ever. Senna, Mansell, Brabham, Scheckter, Clark, Hill, they have all been there. He gelled better than anyone. This is a troubled area with gangs who shoot people. Lewis is the kind of guy who shows kids that if they think a little differently they don't have to go this route. He mixed with everybody and made everybody feel at home. That was a mark of what was coming. I knew he had won in every class, was a very good driver, but this was something special.'

Something special had brewed too for Anthony Hamilton in Barcelona the previous month. It had been the first day of winter testing – that time when drivers put in the miles and log the essential date to extract an advantage in the season ahead. Anthony had spent nearly fifteen years to bring his son to this point. 'It's a proud day. When he got the drive it was the best early Christmas present I could have had. I just wanted to be here to see it. I'm here tomorrow too, and then that'll be it. I'm not for hanging around. Besides, he's the one driving the car.'

The subject of testing also allowed Lewis his first retort to former McLaren employee David Coulthard who had made his belief public that the new British F1 racer would have been better served spending a year testing before committing himself to the race track: 'In some ways he could be right but I've done all I need to do coming up to F1. I have plenty of time to do testing in pre-season. This has been my ambition since a young age. There is no pressure on me to win. I am young, fresh and extremely determined to do well in this sport. I want to win.'

There were, of course, other perspectives on the decision by McLaren. Former World Champion Jacques Villeneuve was quick to offer an opinion: 'He's quick, but still green. He's won everything he's gone into, but that is not always a good thing for F1. But he could buck a trend. He's a very nice character, but since he's the first black driver in F1 a huge amount of pressure and attention will be on him. Any mistake will be heavily criticised, so that will make or break him. Alonso will either make him better or eat him alive. That will depend on how strong Hamilton is himself, but he seems to have good work ethics. McLaren always protect their drivers too, so he should have plenty of time to get up to pace without too much pressure.'

The sagacious Peter Windsor, the Grand Prix editor of *F1 Racing* magazine perceived: 'A driver pairing even greater than Ferrari's. Fernando Alonso is devastatingly good all round and will relish his new challenges at McLaren. And his teammate is Lewis Hamilton, if you please – a rookie intelligent enough to play the number two role, yet quick and aggressive enough to be right there from day one.

These two will win races even if the McLaren is slightly off the pace. In every event they have the mix of personality and energy to take McLaren back to the front.'

Adrian Sutil of the Spyker team provided a personal insight: 'When I was racing for the ASM F3 Euro Series in 2005 with Lewis Hamilton as my teammate, I suffered from nerves a lot. I wasn't confident. Even though Lewis was a little younger than me, he was more experienced. He was usually quicker. He's had so much more experience – karting against the world's best karters from a very young age – and whereas I'd sometimes been in mediocre cars, Lewis always had the best. And, of course, he's always been able to rely on the backing of McLaren and Ron Dennis. He was so confident and in such a good way.'

Tony Purnell was also very much in Lewis's corner: 'Didn't we hear a lot of mutterings about it being "too early for Lewis"; about a McLaren race drive putting him under "too much pressure"; about the theory that "Lewis should spend a year testing before he gets a race drive" because "he's too young". He's been racing as a professional for well over ten years now and he's more than ready.'

Ex-Formula One racer and ITV pundit Mark Blundell reinforced this view: 'Lewis is the first of a new breed of racing driver. There are a number of reasons for this. One, he has unbelievable talent. Two, he is the product of the most professional schooling programme any driver has experienced. Hamilton's ten-year association with McLaren will force teams to reassess their young driver programmes. No one, to my knowledge, has ever been brought on like this. What looked like a heck of a risk ten years ago to start supporting a kid through karts is looking inspired now.'

What did the preparation that Mark Blundell referred to involve? It was the countless hours spent inside the super-simulator that sits in a high-security area at the McLaren team's £500 million technical centre in Woking, Surrey. Lewis was also under the influence of Dr Kerry Spackman who specialises in neuroscience and was introduced to F1 by Sir Jackie Stewart, who got him interested in the functioning of a racing driver's mind. With a racing driver, Dr Spackman aims to increase the brain's muscle power and in particular its storage capacity: 'Memory is a critical aspect of the modern racing driver. When you go into a corner, you do a number of things and the car will respond in a number of ways. You need to store all that in your brain because unless you can store the consequences of everything you've done, you won't be able to analyse them and know what to do next. So if you want to increase a driver's memory for motion, there are certain things you can do to build up those parts of the brain and help it identify even finer detail. And what you can do is give him a process that helps him develop it.'

The process can be carried out in the simulator, or by virtual reality through a process of verbal reconstruction. As a result of this training, when Lewis faces an emergency, 'He probably has twenty-five solutions in his mind. He's exceptionally well prepared. Most people turn up and drive and just deal with situations as they occur. He has the structure to handle it.'

So no wonder the confidence was flowing as well as the wine at the Valencia Opera House for the unveiling of the 2007 McLaren. Lewis was his usual circumspect but upbeat self at this occasion: 'In F1 you have to take your time to learn. It's been a great experience so far. I just want to do a solid job and learn as much as I can from Fernando. He brings so much to the team. But I'm such a strong competitor. Whatever I do I want to be up against the best and beat the best.'

The reigning World Champion welcomed the appointment despite having learnt his trade initially at the back of the grid with Minardi: 'Lewis has a fantastic opportunity to drive a winning car. He comes into F1 with fresh ideas, a new mentality. Sometimes this is what teams need, to change their philosophy a little bit. I started in a smaller team. That way you learn and get experience with no pressure. And when you need the results in a big team you arrive ready. If you start in a big team you need the results straight away. Lewis just has to be as calm as he can, to focus hard when he is in the car. He is a clever guy, I'm sure he'll have no problems.'

Tony Purnell had some interesting words to cast in Fernando Alonso's direction as the season became imminent: 'Lewis didn't smash his way to the top echelon. He danced, waltzed, weaved and dazzled his way there. So he's unlikely to shatter a huge amount of McLaren carbon fibre and he's expected to be seriously outperformed by his double World Champion teammate. Thus, all the expectations, all the pressures, are actually located in the other MP4-22, not Lewis's. If he managed to match or even beat Fernando on occasions – the result will be instant, unequivocal megastardom. Sounds to me like an ideal position to be in.'

Chapter Three

BATTLE JOINED

Lewis Hamilton admitted he could not have expected anything better from his first-ever qualifying session in the sport after he finished fourth at the Albert Park in Melbourne, Australia.

The twenty-two-year-old had impressed throughout his practice sessions ahead of his debut Grand Prix. He showed no signs of nerves as he took to the track for qualifying and challenged at the top throughout. He even threatened a shock pole position until a blip on his final lap meant he finished fourth, with Ferrari's Kimi Räikkönen claiming pole and teammate Fernando Alonso second.

Lewis was delighted with his performance, dismissing suggestions that he was disappointed at not taking pole: 'I think you have to be realistic. It is my first qualifying session and this is the pinnacle of the sport. I am with some of the best drivers in the world. It is not a sport you can come into and go straight to the front, so I absolutely did not expect to get pole. I was just really happy for second row in my first qualifying session. It is more than I could have asked for.'

Fernando Alonso was also pleased by what he had seen from his rookie teammate: 'I think he has been doing a fantastic job so far. He has been competing in all practice sessions and in qualifying also. He can score many points for the team if everything keeps going in his direction.'

Lewis continued: 'The session went very well. For me it was another stepping stone. We didn't seem to have any problems. The car felt quite good. I got some clean laps and I didn't have any mistakes, no offs, and I managed to finish and maximise every lap.

'The team have prepared me very well. They have put together a really good programme to prepare me physically. Mentally, I prepare myself. I have not found myself coming here and going: "Wow, I was not expecting that." Everything went to plan.'

McLaren managing director Martin Whitmarsh confirmed that the young Briton's Grand Prix arrival was plotted as meticulously as one of his famous overtaking moves. For McLaren had designed a schedule which plotted every second of his days for the months leading from his private confirmation in the previous autumn to this debut in Australia in March. 'We set out a plan for him that covered every hour of the day for those six months. It was intensive and he worked amazingly hard at it. That kind of focus makes him the driver he is.' The young man had learned in detail about the engine, the electronics, clutch, tyres, aerodynamics, and spent hundreds of hours in the simulator. 'We wanted to make sure he knew everything about a Grand Prix car,' said Whitmarsh.

Martin had known Lewis for the full nine years of his association with the McLaren team. He had been a prime mover in the protégé's appointment to the race seat. But even he was amazed by Lewis's management of his first outing at the highest level. 'Lewis came to a circuit that is low grip at the best of times, wet on Friday. The first time he had ever driven on an extreme wet tyre coincided with his first lap as a professional racing driver on a circuit that he had never driven. If you get it wrong here, it's quite unforgiving. He progressed from extreme wets to wets, then did one lap on dry. Look at his times. Bang. Straight away he was there. Quick. In the second practice session you had red flags, a bit of drizzle. He dealt with all the issues. I was listening to him on the radio, amazed at how articulate, intelligent and insightful he was.'

Ron Dennis was eventually asked to describe his emotions as he stood next to the young man's car on the Melbourne grid: 'To be honest, apart from the obvious thoughts – things like hoping that both Fernando and he would get through the first corner without incident, which you always hope for with any of your drivers in any race – I was really feeling for him. I could see the pressure on his face. Not much, but some and the few words I shared with him were therefore more paternal than technical or strategic.'

In the race itself, Kimi Räikkönen for Ferrari took a dominant lights-to-flag victory but it was the British debutant who stole the show.

While the Finn got his career off to an expected good start, Lewis's remarkable drive to third place electrified everyone watching at the circuit and far beyond on television. The twenty-two-year-old repaid the faith of the McLaren hierarchy and served notice of his intent by racing his successful teammate for second place all afternoon. The Spaniard finally prevailed after Lewis was delayed by traffic and a slower pit stop, but it was a close-run affair.

By finishing third, the young Briton became the first driver to make it onto the podium on his F1 debut since Jacques Villeneuve in 1996. He also became the third British driver to finish third or better on his Grand Prix debut – the others being Peter Arundell, third in Monaco in 1964, and Mike Parkes, second in France in 1966.

At the start, pole-sitter Räikkönen made a perfect getaway while fellow front-runner Alonso was passed by Nick Heidfeld of BMW on the run to the first corner. Lewis was momentarily trapped behind the fast-starting Robert Kubica but darted around the BMW and then Alonso himself going into the first chicane.

The Flying Finn stamped his authority on the race, building a two-second lead in the first two laps. It was on the seventh lap that Lewis made his first mistake of the weekend, running wide at turn twelve and taking his left-side wheels onto the grass. But the MP4-22 was back on the asphalt quickly and young Hamilton recovered to set a personal-best lap next time around. With BMW having opted to start Heidfeld on the softer of the two tyre compounds, the German was able to keep the McLarens comfortably at bay through the opening stint. However, on lap fifteen Heidfeld initiated the first round of pit stops and briefly dropped to seventh place. That promoted Lewis Hamilton to second, with Alonso around 1.5 seconds back in third. The Ferrari driver out front continued to add to his lead with each new lap, stretching it to 15 seconds by the time he entered the pits for his first stop on lap nineteen. The McLarens were fuelled for a longer opening stint than any of the other front-runners which meant that Lewis Hamilton now joined the elite band of drivers to lead their debut Grand Prix. Fernando Alonso pitted one lap before his teammate, allowing the rookie to rejoin still in second place and with a slightly reduced deficit of 11.6 seconds to Kimi Räikkönen. Räikkönen was under no pressure and soon increased his advantage, assisted by a minor slip from Lewis in turn fourteen.

At the halfway mark the order was Räikkönen, Hamilton, Alonso, Kubica, Heidfeld and Fisichella of Renault. Räikkönen, though, was in a race of his own and posted a series of blistering laps, these culminated in a stunning 1:25.235 on lap fourteen, which was to prove the afternoon's fastest.

Meanwhile, the battle for second was hotting up. The British racer maintained a cushion of around 1.5 seconds over the Spanish racer until his in-lap, when he was held up by the lapped Super Aguri of Takumu Sato and the gap disappeared. With the World Champion staying out for another two laps on a light fuel load, Hamilton's second place looked vulnerable and so it proved. After just 6.5 seconds stationary in the pits, Fernando rejoined comfortably ahead of his teammate and set off in pursuit of the second spot on the podium. Having had a couple of offs earlier in the race as he pushed his McLaren to the very limit, Lewis seemed to tone his driving down in the final stint and looked forward to being on the podium.

He did immediately admit that he was shocked with that podium finish: 'I think this is probably beyond my dreams. To be in Formula One was obviously a dream, but to come to your first race and have such a smooth start is something you don't expect, but something we had been working towards.'

He also admitted that the pressure of having the world number one on his tail for most of the race was no different to anywhere else on the track: 'It's pretty much like that every time you're in that position in a race, whether it's your teammate, you're leading the race or you're trying to catch the guy in front. It's extremely intense, you've got to make sure you make no mistakes – and for sure, I did make a few mistakes in this one. But again, it's another new experience. As I said, I'm ecstatic to be here, a podium for my first race, I couldn't be more happy.'

Ron Dennis was pretty pleased too: 'He drove a great race and afterwards I was utterly delighted for him that all his hard work had been rewarded. The thing that impressed me most about the way he tackled the first corner is that he had the discipline to lift, ever so slightly. Many rookies, particularly starting from P4, would have kept their foot in and got involved in a wheel-banging incident with Nick Heidfeld, who had braked immediately in front of Lewis, but he had the composure to lift and take another route. Perhaps, unexpectedly, in so doing, he then found himself alongside Fernando. What followed was, by Fernando's own admission, a very clean manoeuvre but it made life difficult for us because we didn't appreciate at the time that one of Lewis's front-wing endplates had been slightly damaged. As a result he was struggling a little with understeer.'

Martin Whitmarsh, as ever, had an interesting perspective: 'Lewis exceeded all our expectations. Great drivers always find a little bit more. This weekend has been truly remarkable. He has absolute greatness. Lewis has come to a team of massive expectations. The pressure that comes with that is incredible. If he'd have flopped here we know what the headlines would have been.'

His father's reaction was understandable: 'The emotions are just absolutely incredible. I knew we were going to be in trouble the moment we arrived here this week because Lewis was just so happy. Whenever he is that happy I know there is something special to come. Nothing surprises me with Lewis. The move at the start was classic Lewis. All those years in karting paid off in that one corner. This whole rollercoaster ride, there are not enough superlatives to explain it. This is a fantastic milestone. Sixth would have been great. Third… bloody hell!'

That was the correct insight of family and friends but the greater accolade was surely that of others. Pat Symonds, the Renault head of engineering, commented: 'He was absolutely fantastic. I know the result sheet says that Fernando beat him but I think those who can read a race well will know this was not necessarily the case. All credit to Lewis, to me he had it in the bag. I think he could well have beaten Fernando.' Others joined in, Sir Stirling Moss, Sir Jackie Stewart, triple World Champion Nikki Lauda and Britain's last World Champion, Damon Hill, who stated: 'His start was just a classic, fantastic – pulling that move on the first corner. It was brave but committed. In the race he was pushing. He was confident and he never looked ragged. It was good and I think he's done a bloody good job. He was in the race at the sharp end and was competitive with his teammate. Tremendous.'

Chapter Four

EASTERN PROMISE

Lewis had been travelling around Australia with German driver Adrian Sutil, whose debut for Spyker was less auspicious as he finished a predictable last. The pair took a short break in Thailand before testing resumed at the Sepang circuit ahead of the following month's Grand Prix. By now, young Hamilton was as hot a topic as the region's weather.

Not that this really concerned Adrian: 'We went on holiday and made a hash of playing golf. Lewis had had a few lessons but I hadn't and I managed to ruin a golf club, but it was fun. We just hung out together and relaxed and listened to music.'

The serious business began on 7 April with the qualifying session for the Malaysian Grand Prix. Fernando Alonso qualified second with a time of 1:35.310, whilst Lewis Hamilton's time of 1:36.045 put him fourth on the grid in only his second Formula One race and equalled his qualifying position from the Australian Grand Prix. He commented afterwards: 'The car is working well and I think we could have had two cars on the front row. However, when I came to turn seven it had started spitting with rain a little bit. I had experienced this at the test last week and knew it could be slippery, so I eased off a small amount. Apart from that everything went smoothly and I'm confident for the race tomorrow. I'm on the clean side of the track and will aim to make a good start.' Well, quite an understatement as events proved, for both McLaren drivers led from the third corner with Lewis passing both Ferraris. It was, in fact, the newcomer who reinforced Alonso's victory by holding back the chasing Ferraris and building a buffer during the first stage of the race. It eventually proved comfortable for the leading Spaniard, who took victory 20 seconds ahead of his team partner. Not so comfortable for the youngster who had to fight off Felipe Massa before his first stop and Kimi Räikkönen during the closing stages of the race. He had previously received a front-wing adjustment in his first stop, then set the fastest lap while running a two-lap lighter fuel load than Alonso. His real problems began in the third stint when he struggled on the hard tyres just as Räikkönen was beginning to fly. The Finn had a new set of tyres for his last stint, and the F2007 prefers them to old tyres. Lewis finished just under a second ahead of the Finn. A gap of 9.6 seconds was whittled down to 0.7 over the closing fifteen laps. Massa finished behind Nick Heidfeld of BMW, with Sauber in fifth after a costly off-track excursion before his first pit stop while chasing Hamilton. The Brazilian misjudged his braking into turn four, losing 5.5 seconds, allowing Räikkönen and Heidfeld to get through.

For the Woking team it was their first one-two finish since the Brazilian Grand Prix of 2005. McLaren now led Ferrari by 9 points in the Constructors' Championship with Alonso leading Räikkönen by two points in the Drivers' Championship.

Of the race, Lewis offered the following analysis: 'That's the most difficult race I've ever had. To see two Ferraris behind you, knowing they are quicker than you, it's very difficult to keep them behind. In Australia I had Fernando behind me but he was not breathing down my neck as hard as Felipe and Kimi. Defending is ten times harder than trying to overtake. It was extremely hot in the cockpit. I ran out of water, and I was getting hotter and hotter. It was tricky and I had to keep pushing to the last lap.'

His team boss was full of praise: 'Fernando delivers a wealth of experience and racing capability whilst Lewis continues to demonstrate why he has warranted the enthusiasm of all of us who have worked with him over the years. Everybody throughout our entire organisation deserves to celebrate the success that they have achieved tonight, but of course our attention will quickly turn to the challenge of the next race in Bahrain.'

Lewis Hamilton entered the Kingdom of Bahrain as the most talked about driver in Formula One. In the Gulf the demands were to be more onerous since Bahrain owns thirty per cent of the McLaren team. Whilst others enjoyed some relaxation, Messrs Alonso and Hamilton were required to mix in Bahrain's royal enclosure.

Meanwhile, Ron Dennis had a positive perspective on the season's third race: 'Lewis is a very good all-round talent but he has also got a double World Champion as his team-mate. As you could see after the race in Malaysia, they were delighted for each other and if we can maintain that team spirit through the season we will have a great year.'

So the atmosphere at a team who failed to record a win in 2006 was being transformed by the arrival of Alonso and Hamilton. None, including Ferrari, had posted as many Grand Prix victories as McLaren in the previous quarter-century. McLaren had the opportunity again as they rode with the youngest pairing in the sport.

Prior to qualifying, Lewis admitted his surprise at the start he had made to his career at the highest level and urged caution among those betting on a maiden win. 'I think you have to put things in perspective. Yes, I have two podium finishes but I still have a lot to learn. There is a huge amount to learn from Fernando and the team. There are major challenges ahead that might take me by surprise.'

Soon Lewis and Fernando would start the Bahrain Grand Prix from second and fourth positions respectively. Lewis set a time of 1.32.935 so, in only his third Grand Prix, would start from the front row for the first time. Fernando's time was 1.33.192, putting him on the second row.

Lewis was more than pleased: 'It just keeps getting better and better – to be on the front row in only my third Formula One weekend is an amazing feeling. I don't think that my final qualifying lap was my best lap of the session.

Qualifying is so intense and you need to pull out everything. The wind also keeps changing direction here which makes things even more challenging. It looks like all the hard work has paid off, and we have definitely closed the gap to Ferrari and made progress. The start tomorrow will be crucial – there is a very long run down into the first corner. However, I have raced here at this circuit before so I have a bit more experience than the last two races and we will see what happens.'

The stakes were raised by Felipe Massa, who had edged the twenty-two-year-old Briton to take pole position for the second successive race, insisting he would be aggressive on the first corner in the race. Lewis was to respond: 'It is intimidating. I think he is attempting to play some mind games but it makes no difference to me, I know what I will do. For sure I have to be aware, if he is to be a little more aggressive then it could be dangerous. I want to make the first lap and score as many points as I can.'

Lewis had last competed in Bahrain in 2004 as a Formula Three driver, shooting from the back of the grid to score an outstanding victory: 'I think I started twenty-third but it was a two-part race and was eleventh on the grid for the second heat. Circumstances were very different then because I had a slightly lucky first lap, but this is a completely different kettle of fish.'

So for the first time in his Formula One career he would be racing on a circuit with which he was familiar and if he finished in the top three Lewis would become the first driver in the World Championship's fifty-eight-year-old history to achieve consecutive podium finishes in his first three Grand Prix.

Eventually, Ferrari's Felipe Massa held off the challenge of Lewis Hamilton to win his first race of the season. The Brazilian led comfortably into the first corner, but could not shake the Briton from his rear-view mirrors during the first part of the race. By the time of the McLaren driver's first stop for fuel on lap nineteen, the Ferrari was still only around a second ahead, but the stops had an influence. Hamilton found his car lacking grip on his new tyres and Massa began to pull away. From pressuring the lead Ferrari, Lewis now came under pressure from Räikkönen. The Finn had spent the first stint stuck behind Alonso, but after passing the Spaniard during the first pits stops he set about trying to make good the damage. As in Malaysia, the young Englishman defended like a driver of greater experience, and despite making a final stop three laps later than the Finnish driver, Lewis managed to rejoin the circuit remaining in second place.

Fernando Alonso could not get anywhere near his junior partner. The Spaniard struggled to master the car under braking. It was Lewis Hamilton who took the fight to Ferrari. Five times in the opening stint, on laps eight, nine, fifteen, seventeen and eighteen, Lewis set the fastest lap. He was quickest, too, in the final phase of the race. Had the used tyres in the second stint performed adequately, McLaren believed that their protégé could have been celebrating his first victory in Bahrain.

Backstage, preparing for the media commitments, Lewis spoke to his Brazilian opponent: 'Ten more laps and I would have given you a race.' Felipe replied: 'Yeah, but I was taking it easy. I was saving the car.' They each laughed and enjoyed a moment of rapport.

The result left Alonso, Räikkönen and Hamilton in a three-way tie on 22 points at the top of the world standings, with Massa five behind. Exclaimed Lewis: 'To have the same points as the others is fantastic. I am extremely proud of that. We have worked extremely hard for this for the last thirteen years. Me and my family. And the team. Now I am looking forward to going home. I have been away for nine weeks. I know the support is growing at home but I have not experienced it yet. I just hope that I can still walk on the streets!'

On the podium, the joy of Massa and Hamilton was there for all to see. There was respect and warmth between them as well. The race itself was becoming a distillation of the season with the advantage ebbing and flowing between the leaders. Commented the history-maker: 'I knew that he was going a lap more than me. I had to stay as close behind him as possible. I think we were fairly well matched. If we had been in front we would have pulled away. Usually the Ferrari has the pace to pull away so I think we have made a fantastic step forward.'

However, the World Champion later complained of grip problems, saying he had 'no confidence' in the car and after his first stop he quickly came under pressure from Nick

Heidfeld of BMW Sauber who grabbed fourth place. It seemed to observers that Lewis Hamilton had disturbed his teammate's equilibrium, especially when Ron Dennis wrapped a reassuring arm around the number one in that Bahrain paddock and proffered: 'We are privileged to have the double World Champion in the car and the chemistry between the two is fantastic. We in Bahrain were just talking about life in general. It was a kind of paternal touch. Fernando and Lewis are passionate people, different characters and it is very easy to work with them. There is not an issue between them and we'll make sure it stays that way. We want to win the World Championship. We have the young pretender and the champion and we owe it to them to give them equal opportunity.'

The team blamed themselves for holding both back. It was claimed they had not given Alonso a good enough car, and that they had made a mistake with tyre pressures and the front-wing settings during Hamilton's first pit stop.

Away from McLaren's investigation into that, there was still time to join in a chorus of appreciation for their up-and-coming superstar. Martin Whitmarsh even went so far as to suggest that Lewis Hamilton might become the greatest driver of all time: 'Since I joined McLaren in 1989 I've worked with a lot of great drivers including Alain Prost, Ayrton Senna, Mika Häkkinen, Kimi Räikkönen and now Fernando Alonso with Lewis, and I think I've developed a pretty clear picture of what gives the top guys that crucial edge over the simply good or average drivers. And I think it is pretty clear that Lewis ticks all the necessary boxes.'

The McLaren chief executive continued that to be one of the very best a driver had: 'to assemble a selection of components. Firstly, and obviously, you need the natural skill. Secondly, you require a considerable degree of natural toughness. Thirdly, some technical empathy is a major benefit because it helps a driver to integrate better with his engineers, which in turn speeds up the car development progress. Finally, there is fitness, determination and application.'

With Sir Jackie Stewart having reached the top of the podium in only his eighth race, he could recognise a precocious talent and as early as this stage was predicting the ultimate prize within time for the young Englishman: 'It's not inconceivable that it could be done this year because McLaren look like the team to beat. If not, expect it in the next three.'

Sir Jackie added: 'He is, of course, driving for one of the best teams in the world at the present time, with a competitive car, but nevertheless he's been able to accomplish more in a shorter time than any driver I've ever seen.'

Another knight of the realm, Frank Williams, was to describe the achievement of recording three successive podium finishes in a debut season as 'superhuman': 'I thought after we got rid of Michael Schumacher, now we've got a chance again. But then another superhuman turns up. Michael was many things but he was also a very simple human. Hamilton is a different character, I think, but, purely in terms of calibre or quality of skill, what I'm seeing so early in this man's career is remarkable.'

Bernie Ecclestone – F1's commercial rights holder – was hooked:'I hope he'll be the next superstar of Formula One. He's got all the makings. He's done an awful lot better than anybody expected him to do. He's young, good-looking and he talks to people. He's selling the business 100 per cent.'

McLaren were actually becoming anxious that Lewis's profile was burgeoning too quickly, and that before long it might grow well beyond the control of their very protective media management team. Certainly the British papers were devoting major column inches to Formula One again and ITV were delighted with the upsurge in viewing figures.

Lewis's successes, by Barcelona, had put him on the front page of two UK dailies and this reflected the amount of Formula One coverage across the UK print media. Media research company Sports Marketing Surveys (SMS) reported that F1 column inches in UK newspapers were seventy per cent up year on year. This at a time when there had been the closest Premiership football climax for years; there were three teams in the UEFA Champions League semi-finals; plus the opening of the new Wembley Stadium for high-profile events. The company also indicated that although TV audiences for the first three races were down year on year by 9.4 per cent, the actual ITV race highlights after Bahrain were up by seventy-three per cent on 2006.

The BBC also featured in the sense that Lewis topped a preliminary poll for the BBC Sports Personality of the Year, with forty-four per cent of voters on the BBC Sports website picking young Hamilton ahead of tennis star Andy Murray on twenty-three per cent and boxer Joe Calzaghe on eleven per cent.

The acclaim proved international too. According to Google trends, searches for Lewis Hamilton were highest as a proportion of total Google searches in Hungary, followed by the UK, then Spain and Finland. This effect was not confined to Europe. In Colombia some thirty-five minutes of a popular motor sport TV show were devoted to the British driver. What made this particular Columbian broadcast so noteworthy was that Juan Pablo Montoya was competing in a live Nascar event and received only ninety seconds of reportage at the end of the programme.

Key sponsors were very happy with this profile too. Santander was both a team sponsor and the British Grand Prix title sponsor. They had entered the sport with three objectives in mind. Firstly, to raise awareness of the Spanish banking group's 150th anniversary. Secondly, to raise Santander's status as one of the world's biggest financial institutions. Thirdly, to reinforce the link between the former Abbey National and Santander, who had acquired the British group in 2004.

The success of the McLaren on track and the measurable increase of interest in Lewis Hamilton was excellent news for them, especially in the British marketplace. They decided to reinforce the link between their brand and the driver. They were to feature Lewis in a sixty-second advertisement for Abbey's current account. He had appeared in TV commercials before for McLaren's title sponsor Vodafone. However, Santander pushed matters further by involving Lewis out of the car and delivering a voiceover. It was recognition that the young man was a celebrity, not only a racing driver. The campaign was backed up by marketing displays at point of sale with all of Abbey's 750 UK branches. By normal standards Lewis Hamilton had certainly arrived.

This also demonstrated the potential downside for someone like Andrew Franzak. As sports editor of the *Hertfordshire Mercury Newspaper* he had covered the twenty-two-year-old's exploits for the past decade. Now with everyone wanting a piece of the rising star, Lewis's words and movements were becoming restricted. Andrew commented: 'This time last year when Lewis was racing in GP2 I just picked up the telephone and he would be on the end of the line. There is very little chance of that happening now, even having established a rapport with Lewis and his dad Anthony. That's the main difference – everything has to go through McLaren now. They've put a tight ring around him.'

Chapter Five

EUROPEAN UNION

Lewis Hamilton was now confident he would win his first Grand Prix in his first season as he looked to keep his astonishing title tilt on track. He had already secured a place in the sport's history books by finishing on the podium in his first three races.

The twenty-two-year-old Briton saw no reason why he could not fight for the crown over the remaining fourteen races, and that certainly he would take the chequered flag at some stage – maybe even at the Circuit de Catalunya. 'I definitely never imagined I would be a joint leader in the Drivers' Championship at this stage,' said Lewis. 'Going into your first season you don't expect that. It was only last year I was watching the Grand Prix. It is unreal. But it is also very cool and I am enjoying it. It shows our true pace, and I hope that I can continue to score points and build on the start to the season.

'You have to have the belief you can succeed in order to ensure you have the commitment, which is true for anything in any walk of life. As long as we continue having one of the leading cars and the team continues to be one of the top two then there is no reason why we can't challenge for the constructors' and drivers' titles.

'We need to keep what we have, to work on the reliability of the car and make sure we don't have any DNFs and focus on pushing forward performance.'

Asked if he felt he would win his first race that season, Lewis simply replied: 'Yes.' He then added: 'I don't want that to come across as a cocky answer. It is just my feeling.' His clear aim was to try and do that in Spain as he commented further: 'I never go with expectations. I go with a target. That is to be at the front, and the ultimate aim is to win, which is the mentality I have always gone racing with.'

Plenty of pundits had suggested that Hamilton could win at least one race that season but Niki Lauda, himself a three-time World Champion, believed that the newcomer could go all the way: 'As unbelievable as it sounds, at the moment I can see Lewis Hamilton heading the ranking. Because of his young and clean experience – he is as fast as Alonso.'

The Austrian, who was champion in 1975, 1977 and 1984, was expecting the unfolding season to be a classic: 'This season will be the most exciting for years. We will not only see a shoot-out between the teams, but also amongst the teammates,' he continued. 'There will be a do-or-die fight between Alonso and Hamilton, and between Massa and Räikkönen. I hope they will not give any team orders until the last two races. At the moment I cannot see a faster driver within either of these teams.'

However, leading up to Barcelona, Lewis was attempting to keep his feet on the ground. He headed for the sanctuary of the family home after his heroics, spending time playing computer games with his brother, who has cerebral palsy. 'We recently bought a PS3 and new F1 game. I have to be Kimi, as there isn't a game with me in yet. My brother is very competitive – and, yes, sometimes he wins, but I'm very competitive too. So he has to win fair and square.' However, it was not all about healthy competition with his sibling: 'I'm seven years older than Nicolas. We're very close and we talk all the time. He's an inspiration. He never complains, always smiles, keeps his chin up, and gets on with life. There's a strong message which has influenced my approach to life. If I ever start to think about the turns my life has taken I think about Nicolas and that keeps me real. My learning curve has been nothing compared to his.'

At the end of his domestic bliss he was due at the McLaren factory in Woking: 'I've relocated to be close to the team. I train every day in the gym and prepare in the simulator.' The offer of a chauffer was turned down. He travelled in on the train and the tube with his father. There seemed a determination by his parents to resist the celebrity culture despite the constant media references to his star qualities. 'You can say that, but I don't feel it. I feel like an F1 driver. So if that means I'm a superstar, then so be it. I just feel great to be here. I'm living the dream.' That balanced view seemed to place Lewis in the right frame of mind: 'Time with the family has been great. Last weekend we had a good fifty people at home. I told them that I wanted to be treated as I always have been. I'm still Lewis. It's important for me to have that bond.' Again he paid tribute to his father: 'If I didn't keep on the ground my dad would kick my arse. He's always been there for me. It is him and my family that keep me grounded.'

This didn't mean that once Lewis set foot in Spain he wasn't able to switch into another compartment in his mind: 'I come as a known competitor. Before, I was just seen as the rookie coming into the sport. Now they can see what I can do. They can see that I can actually drive.'

Young Hamilton would have at his disposal a car with a new front wing. McLaren had added an element that connected to the end plates and bridged the nose. The gain in speed would be needed as Ferrari had been busy making improvements too. Things could scarcely be closer.

Eventually, Fernando Alonso and Lewis Hamilton would start the Grand Prix from second and fourth positions respectively with Felipe Massa on his third consecutive pole and Kimi Räikkönen in third place. Fernando set a time of 1:21.451 and was just 0.030 seconds from pole position. Lewis's fastest time was 1:21.785.

'I was quite happy with my lap,' the young Briton reported. 'I don't think I could have gone a great deal faster – one tenth of a second, perhaps, but no more. Today, though, I didn't have a car that was quick enough for the front row.' How did this compare with his teammate? 'We were on different fuel loads and I believe I have a strong race strategy.' The next day he would attempt to extend the record of podium finishes that had made him the most successful World Championship newcomer since the series began in 1950.

It would also have to be a big day for Fernando Alonso at his home Grand Prix in front of his adoring fans. Many felt that he needed a performance to reassert his authority within the team and many more were surprised that his position was under challenge at all. Sir Jackie Stewart claimed that Lewis's emergence had introduced a ragged edge to his driving: 'He missed the apex of one turn completely this morning. He made three big mistakes. He was over-driving. After the first mistake he should have backed off. Instead he compounded it by carrying on. Usually he is so smooth. I don't think there is any question that Alonso is feeling it. Hamilton's brilliant start has definitely given him something to think about.'

One can only imagine what was going through Alonso's mind when at the conclusion of the race Lewis Hamilton had again rewritten the sport's history book. In following Felipe Massa past the chequered flag ahead of his teammate, Lewis at twenty-two years, four months and six days became the youngest driver to ever lead the Formula One World Championship. Ironically, it was Bruce McLaren who had held that distinction since 1960. Lewis led with 30 points – two more than his teammate.

The Brazilian winner had benefited from a coming-together with Alonso, with the home driver ending up in the gravel and dropping two places to fourth. Meanwhile, Lewis had already seen off Kimi Räikkönen with Alonso's aggression providing a bonus. Once into a quick second place, his McLaren was off in pursuit of the leading Ferrari. With a lighter fuel load, Massa was away. Later, Ron Dennis was to admit that a wrong choice of tyre – the harder compound over the softer – gave Ferrari a further advantage during the second stint.

Afterwards, Lewis remained upbeat: 'I keep saying I'm living my dream. It's true. To come into my fourth Grand Prix and come out of it leading the championship it is just incredible. I could not be happier. I came into the season with an open mind, but never felt this was possible. I just hoped I would come in and do a good job. I have been working so many years for this. The whole thing is getting bigger and bigger. I'm going to be gunning for the win in Monaco.'

At this point there was much speculation that Lewis Hamilton and not Fernando Alonso could become the first McLaren World Champion since Mika Häkkinen. Of course, no rookie had won the championship in his first season. Jacques Villeneuve had set the benchmark for rookie drivers in 1996. Driving for Williams, Villeneuve finished runner-up to teammate Damon Hill in the championship, setting rookie records for points with a total of 78 plus four race wins and eleven podium appearances. On his status as a newcomer, Lewis was clear: 'I am a rookie and there's a lot to learn. I need to improve in a lot of areas. I don't think there is a limit. Any driver can improve. I think even Michael Schumacher was improving.'

The Briton's confidence about the impending street circuit was based on empiric evidence: 'Monaco has always been a very strong race for me. It is one of the tracks I have always dreamed of racing in F1. However, I do have to keep being realistic. This is my fifth race in F1 and I am still developing. I have to focus on keeping scoring points for both championships and take it step by step.'

While Monaco was traditionally viewed as a real test for F1 newcomers, it was obvious that he was relishing the opportunity: 'I am really looking forward to it. For me, it's the best circuit of the year; there is nowhere like it for getting the adrenalin flowing. Because there are no run-off areas you have to be incredibly precise. There is no room for error and that makes it all the more exciting.'

However, the Mercedes Motorsport boss Norbert Haug attempted to keep matters in perspective: 'It's not right to describe him as the big favourite for Monaco. He has been exceptional to be second three times in a row and has had fantastic races there in the past. He is a street racer but maybe the focus is on him too much. McLaren should be in good shape but Ferrari is still slightly faster. Hopefully we can apply the pressure.'

Lewis no doubt applied some psychological pressure when testing took place at Paul Ricard in France. Here, in a configuration centred on 27 May's race around the streets of Monte Carlo, the McLaren rookie lapped the

3.593km circuit in a time of 1:05.614. His best effort placed him 0.141 seconds clear of the day's second quickest driver, Ferrari's Felipe Massa. The McLaren team also continued to work on their preparations for the forthcoming Grand Prix, including the aero package of their MP4-22 chassis, Bridgestone Potenza evaluation and set-ups.

After Lewis had completed ninety-eight successful laps, his rival, Massa, was generous in his appraisal: 'It is Hamilton who leads right now and I have spoken quite a bit to him. He is definitely strong and is not bothered by the pressure. At the moment, you cannot say that Fernando or him is the better driver, but if the situation continues like this, then maybe Lewis can be even more dangerous than Fernando.'

Before the action came the traditional glamour of the Monaco setting. Lewis took part in a promotion by diamond trader Steinmetz on the deck of a massive yacht called the *Floridian*, for he and his teammate would race around the Principality with diamonds inlaid along the side of their helmets spelling the words 'Monaco 07'. The young man exclaimed: 'I've got bling on my helmet – how cool is that?'

Not that he wasn't focused. When asked by ITV's Ted Kravitz whether he was up for it and whether he was fit he replied: 'Absolutely, very fit – probably fitter than I have been all season and I'm more relaxed than I have been all season. Already the atmosphere is building up and I'm just really excited to be here on the back of the biggest boat that I think I have ever seen.'

However, Britain's rising sports star was to receive a reality check when his car plunged off the road into the wall during the ninety-minute free practice session on the Friday. Braking hard for the tricky second-gear 60mph Saint Devote right-hander, Lewis went into the outer barrier, ripping off the left-hand front wheel and shuddering to a halt in a cloud of smoke and debris. He strolled calmly from the wreckage and later gave this assessment: 'Today was the first time I ever drove a Formula One car around Monaco and it was awesome. I have obviously had experience around Monaco in a Formula Three and a GP2 car, but in Formula One it is very different. I found out how unforgiving the track can be when I went off in the second session, causing some damage to the car. I'm obviously sorry because there will be a bit of work for the guys but until then everything had been going smoothly and we had been able to set some competitive lap times. I made a small error under braking for Saint Devote, and the tyres hadn't worked up enough grip so I made a tiny mistake, the back of the car slipped and that was it.' Typical honesty from the young driver but that ability to express himself clearly was to lead to complications for his team by the time the weekend was over.

At the end of qualifying it was Fernando Alonso who would claim his first pole position for his new team with his teammate making it an all-McLaren Mercedes front row. Fernando recorded a time of 1:15.726 whilst Lewis did 1:15.905. Lewis offered the following analysis: 'That first lap was very quick with fuel. It was a good lap, and I was fortunate to finish it due to a bit of rain. Then we put the new tyres on, and on my next flying lap I was up by three tenths at Casino Square – turn four. Then I lost half a second behind Webber yet still managed to do exactly the same time. I don't know whether Webber didn't see me, but he said in the drivers' briefing that we need to be hard on people who hold others up, then he came out and held me up.' He later added: 'For my first Grand Prix here, I am really happy to start in second place. I think tomorrow is going to be very interesting.' He also stated that he intended to stay calm and not jeopardise the chances of McLaren scoring a record fourteenth victory at the venue. He was additionally aware of the need to fend off any attacks from Felipe Massa, who was starting from third on the grid, and so he played safe initially and tucked in behind his number one.

In the event Alonso led for the lion's share, Hamilton only popping in front for short periods coming up to his refuelling stops. Felipe Massa finished a distant third and was impressed with the speed of the McLarens: 'Definitely today they showed incredible pace,' said the Brazilian. 'Even if I had pushed 150 per cent it would have changed nothing.'

Fernando crossed the line first with Lewis 4 seconds behind for the team's second one-two finish of the season, lapping the entire field, with the exception of Massa. However, it soon became obvious that a bitter disappointment was etched on the face of the usually ebullient younger driver. What was emerging was that a team known for giving their drivers an equal crack at victory had realised their best purpose on this occasion was not served by the drivers going for each other. Hamilton's racing instincts had been reined in by instructions from above. Team orders had been banned in Formula One since 2002 after Rubens Barrichello was instructed to hand over the lead of that year's Austrian Grand Prix to his Ferrari team leader Michael Schumacher to protect the German driver's World Championship lead.

Lewis was less than a second behind his teammate with twenty of the seventy-eight laps to go, then eased off the throttle. The order not to go for Alonso came earlier, with more than half the race to go. The Briton was brought in prematurely for his second stop, costing him any chance of victory. His reaction was measured: 'I have the number two on my car. I'm the number two driver. At the end of the day I am a rookie coming into my first season, so to finish second in my first Monaco Grand Prix, I can't complain.'

Ron Dennis described his mood and his move: 'We are pleased with the one–two but my job carried difficult decisions. I make no excuses for instructing the drivers to slow their pace after the first stop and to affect our strategy based on the possibility of other cars affecting us if the safety car were deployed. I don't like to slow drivers down; I don't like them to be frustrated; I don't like to see these things happen because I am an absolute racer but that is the way you have to win the Monaco Grand Prix.' Of any future scenario with his protégé, the McLaren principal commented: 'There will be a place where he is absolutely free to race, but this is not one of them.'

Then, on the Monday came the following announcement from the governing body: 'The FIA has launched an investigation into incidents involving the McLaren Mercedes team at the 2007 Monaco Grand Prix in light of a possible breach of the international sporting code.' The media speculated on the risk that Lewis Hamilton's World Championship challenge might be undermined by disqualification from the Monaco Grand Prix if it was proved that McLaren imposed illegal team orders on him. The Federation was expected to examine radio transmissions from the McLaren pit to their two drivers to establish whether instructions to hold position after the second round of refuelling stops amounted to an infraction.

Fernando Alonso was on a two-stop strategy from the outset whereas Lewis Hamilton started with a one-stop plan, carrying five more laps fuel than Alonso. He was brought in for his first refuelling stop only three laps after the Spaniard because he was not close enough to have a chance of resuming in the lead and since he was comfortably second he was switched to a two-stop strategy because it was the fastest option for the balance of the race. In the view of many, McLaren could be forgiven for putting their strategic might behind the World Champion, who on paper offered the greater chance of victory.

Sir Jackie Stewart had a clear opinion in support of the team: 'Alonso was on pole position, he made a very good start, he took a lead that allowed him to have a good, clear bit of air behind him. He set the fastest lap and he won the race. It was fairly straightforward.' The three-times World Champion added: 'It's a very difficult thing to tell team owners that, if you're running first and second, you should keep driving your drivers to the absolute maximum of their ability.'

The argument was that Barrichello handing the victory to Schumacher in season 2002 was different to McLaren safeguarding their drivers. As Ron Dennis proffered: 'At the end of the day, McLaren has now won an all-time record 14 out of 65 races at Monaco. Why? Because McLaren understands better than anybody what's involved in winning races there.'

Eventually, the team were cleared of any wrong-doing when the FIA, meeting in Paris proclaimed: 'Having studied the radio traffic between Vodafone McLaren Mercedes and its drivers, together with the FIA observer's report and data from the team, it is clear that McLaren's actions during the 2007 Monaco Grand Prix were entirely legitimate and no further action is necessary.'

The issue was whether, in ordering their drivers to maintain the status quo, McLaren had interfered with the result? The answer was confirmed by the FIA: 'It is standard procedure for a team to tell its drivers to slow down when they have a substantial lead. This is in order to minimise the risk of technical and other problems. It is also standard practice and entirely reasonable to ask the drivers not to put each other at risk. McLaren were able to pursue an optimum team strategy because they had a substantial advantage over all other cars.'

Whilst Lewis's frustration and disappointment was understandable, it would have to be his quest now to seek pole position in the coming races and gain team support. The McLaren duo headed to North America for back-to-back races in Canada and America as joint leaders of the championship on 38 points, five points clear of Ferrari's Felipe Massa. A fascinating situation was brewing.

Chapter Six

DOUBLE FIRST

Lewis Hamilton was about to begin the toughest phase of his fledgling Formula One career, starting in Canada for the first of four races in the following month. At this point he had recorded a third place and two consecutive second places in a record-breaking sequence. Lewis obviously felt that he might have gone one better in the previous race at Monaco but for the McLaren management's decision to protect their position on track.

The young Briton had the disadvantage of never having raced at Montreal – or for that matter at Indianapolis, the venue a week later. Alonso had been there but not that successfully. The World Champion was now adjusting to Bridgestone tyres after years with Michelin tyres at Renault. Montreal, with its long straights and twisting turns, was known as a heavy-braking circuit and was likely to test Alonso. Under all circumstances Lewis had been at least as quick as his teammate since the Bahrain Grand Prix.

In Lewis's post-race comments at Monte Carlo the young man had made claims about his perceived status that ran contrary to McLaren's stated ethos that drivers were always treated equally. This displayed a frustration yet a competitiveness that was brewing ahead of Montreal.

His arrival in North America also had another controversial note. Local hero Jacques Villeneuve bucked the trend and openly criticised Lewis Hamilton's driving, with particular reference to his aggressive starts: 'When will these chopping moves stop? Lewis is not getting penalised for these things and his behaviour off the start line has started to look the way Michael used to. So far he has been lucky, so we'll see if it carries on,' the former World Champion commented. 'He makes progressive moves that would have got some of the drivers black-flagged. We still haven't seen how he reacts under pressure. That will be interesting to watch.' Cue Lewis Hamilton in response: 'Jacques deserves to have his opinions about it and I can respect that, but this is racing. If you are cutting across people, being dangerous and possibly taking them out, then I would totally agree. But that has not been the case in any of the races I have seen. It has not been dangerous up until now and I think you can see that it is for the FIA to make the choice'

The demand for a sound bite or quote from Lewis was now proving immense. The McLaren motor home was surrounded by microphones and cameras. Lewis, however, was aware that his post-race candour at Monaco had instigated an inquiry by the sport's regulatory body: 'I'm only five races into my F1 career. I'm learning things along the way. It's a steep learning curve. You have to learn. Next time I might watch what I say, but I just said what I felt in

Monaco. I'm only human. Sometimes your feelings need to be expressed so that everybody knows how you feel.'

What was plain after Monaco was that Lewis Hamilton not only had speed, determination and consistency but was presenting the McLaren bosses and his teammate with an earlier-than-anticipated challenge over equal status: 'I think every weekend when I am matching the times and doing as well as if not better than Fernando, I am demonstrating that I've got the ability to be a champion, to deserve at least to be equal. I get the same equipment, a great bunch of guys working with me and I believe I have the best engineer because of the relationship we have built.' However, the most interesting aspect of Lewis's perspective came with his allied comments about Rubens Barrichello at Ferrari in previous times: 'The situation that Rubens was in − if that was ever the case, I wouldn't be here for much longer. Rubens knew that Schumacher was the main man.'

The Circuit Gilles Villeneuve presented new demands for Lewis but he had spent hours 'driving' it on McLaren's simulator: 'I don't know the circuit but I learn quite quickly. There are some long straights and opportunities to overtake. But I don't really plan to do any overtaking. I want to get on the front row and go off and do the business.'

In the first of two sessions, the Briton finished second fastest, just behind Alonso. The Spaniard maintained his superiority in the afternoon session, lapping half a second faster than Felipe Massa's Ferrari. Lewis, meanwhile, struggled with his car set-up on his way to a third fastest lap – three-tenths off the Brazilian but seven-tenths off his team partner. So little clue as to what would yet be achieved.

Then Lewis Hamilton finally got everything right by out-duelling Fernando Alonso for a brilliant maiden Formula One pole position in final qualifying. He set a fastest time of 1:15.707 with Alonso on 1:16.163. It was the second consecutive one-two qualifying of the season for the Vodafone McLaren Mercedes team. The twenty-two-year-old rookie had previously traded times with the World Champion before putting together an exquisite final lap while Alonso made a slight mistake. To say that the British driver was pleased would be an understatement: 'This is the best feeling I have ever had. This is just fantastic. It is another step on my steep learning curve in Formula One. I always knew I had it in me but I was not sure when it was going to happen. But I got the opportunity and this time I grabbed it.' He continued: 'I will have a good night with dad and my trainer, and relax. I will get a good night's sleep and then come back and do the same job in the race. I will have to make sure I have both my mirrors covered and not give up any space at the first corner.' His father, Anthony, added: 'I can't believe what's happened to the family this year. What Lewis has done is incredible.'

Lewis had the previous experience of the simulator but could now offer a perspective of the real thing: 'The circuit took a while to learn in practice. It looks a simple circuit but it is demanding physically and mentally. But when I arrived it was like going out on a circuit you've never been on before. I went away after practice and worked out how I could improve my lap as I knew I had a quicker time in me. The car was so sweet and I didn't make a mistake. But the race is going to be tough and Fernando will be my main rival.'

Lewis admitted that he was on the limit when he obtained the quickest pole by a rookie since Jacques Villeneuve took top spot on his debut in Australia in 1996. It had taken Michael Schumacher 41 races before his first pole, although Lewis was not the quickest British racer to achieve the feat. Former World Champion John Surtees did it in his second race.

'I was chuffed when the team told me I was P1. When you know your lap is going to be quick you come up to that final corner at 210mph and you just think, "Don't mess it up!" But it was tight and it's not easy when you have a two-time World Champion hunting you down – but I did it. I stayed strong today.'

So Lewis – thirty-five years on from Mosport, Canada where Peter Revson had taken McLaren's first pole – had taken one of his own.

On race day the weather was the hottest of the weekend with an air temperature of 27°C. On the track it was 53° when the cars lined up on the grid. The pole-sitter made a clean start to lead the pack into the first corner. His team-mate was less fortunate and in attempting to fend off a fast-starting Heidfeld went right across the grass on the right, rejoining in third place. Räikkönen also fluffed his getaway, losing two places after contact with his teammate.

At the end of lap one, the first six positions were: Hamilton (McLaren), Heidfeld (BMW Sauber), Alonso (McLaren), Massa (Ferrari), Rosberg (Williams-Toyota) and Räikkönen (Ferrari). With four laps gone, Hamilton was four seconds in front of Heidfeld and five ahead of Alonso, with Massa back in fourth, some six seconds behind.

On lap eighteen Alonso made another mistake, under-braking for the first corner, and Massa nipped by into third. Next time around Heidfeld initiated the first round of refuelling stops, followed by the leading McLaren a lap later. Just as Lewis came out, Sutil's Spyker Ferrari hit a wall and brought out the safety car. Alonso and Rosberg were refuelling at that moment. The race neutralisation was good news for those who had already refuelled as they rejoined with all the gaps reduced to zero. Not such good news for Lewis Hamilton.

At the end of lap twenty-five, the pit lane was declared open and those who wished to refuel were free to do so. The green flag was waved on lap twenty-seven with Hamilton, Massa and Alonso tumbling all over each other. A lap later, Robert Kubica's BMW Sauber hit Jarno Truli's Toyota and went off at full speed just before the hairpin. The BMW slammed into the wall, broke up and came back onto the track, rolling over several times before grinding to a halt. Medical help arrived immediately and the safety car came out again. Later on it was announced that Kubica was conscious and in a stable condition after his horrific accident.

The race restarted on lap thirty-three with no changes in the first three, followed by Nico Rosberg, who had not yet stopped like his immediate pursuers Davidson (Super Aguri), Schumacher (Toyota) and Webber (Red Bull). At that moment Alonso went through the pits for a stop-and-go penalty.

With thirty laps to the finish, Hamilton led the race from Heidfeld, Webber, Massa and Fisichella (Renault). At the end of lap forty-seven, Lewis Hamilton came in for his final stop. Meanwhile, Christian Albers (Spyker) went across the grass, losing his front wing and bringing out the safety car for the third time. Now only twenty laps remained. Race control then told Ferrari and Renault that Massa and Fisichella had been excluded for having left the pit lane after their first refuelling stops when the light was still red.

Several drivers, including Räikkönen and Alonso, took advantage of the neutralisation to refuel, and as the two cars left their pits the Spaniard edged ahead of the Finn. However, once again Alonso went grass-cutting when the green light flashed and lost several places. The final twist came when Liuzzi (Toro Rosso) hit the wall just after the last corner and out came the safety car for the fourth time! This certainly added pressure for race-leader Lewis Hamilton.

When the race finally began again there was an interesting order: Hamilton, Heidfeld, Barrichello, Wurz (Williams),

Kovalainen and Räikkönen. Barrichello (Honda) came in to refuel on lap sixty-three while Kovalainen tried all he knew to snatch third place from Wurz. Whilst he was unable to pass the Williams, Takumo Sato (Super Aguri) provided the last-minute thrills by passing both Schumacher and Alonso to finish sixth. When the flag finally fell, the podium was Lewis Hamilton, Nick Heidfeld and Alex Wurz after a memorable Grand Prix in more ways than one.

Not since 1957, when Tony Brooks claimed the British Grand Prix at Aintree in his fourth race, had a home-grown driver won so early in his F1 career and in such style. Triple champion Sir Jackie Stewart took eight races, champion Damon Hill 13, David Coulthard 21, champion James Hunt 30, champion Graham Hill 33, Eddie Irvine 81 and Jenson Button 113.

Lewis's victory in only his sixth Formula One race sparked spontaneous pit-lane celebrations that went beyond his team. The winner whooped with delight as he took the chequered flag and performed a little dance on top of his car before he leapt from it. Two weeks previously in Monte Carlo there had been almost a sense of anti-climax but now there was only fulfilment: 'I'm having a fantastic day, this is historic. I was trying to control myself on the last lap. I just wanted to stop the car and jump out. I've been ready for this for quite some time, ready for the win – it was just a matter of where and when. I have to dedicate this win to my dad – without him this wouldn't have been possible. I saw him when I was on the podium and could see he had a tear in his eye. It felt very emotional.' The tribute was richly deserved and continued: 'You wouldn't believe the amount of work he's put into my career. He had nothing when he was younger. He lost his Mum at a young age and just to see his family be successful is a real pleasure to him.'

It was obvious that the close bond with father Anthony, as well as half-brother Nicolas, had been a force in his meteoric rise. As a young man, Anthony met and married Carmen Larbalestier, naming their son after the American Olympic athlete Carl Lewis. They divorced when he was a toddler and he lived with his father and stepmother. Anthony Hamilton was not born to wealth or privilege like many in motor racing. The story had emerged of how Anthony, whose own father worked on the London Underground and who was himself employed on the railways, juggled three jobs to pay for Lewis's early karting activities.

That background had obviously kept the rookie's feet on the ground and provided a sense of perspective. This and the family factor had been witnessed in Monaco the previous month. After taking his trophy from Prince Albert, Lewis stepped down and handed it to Nicolas, watching from a wheelchair. At the time Lewis commented: 'My brother supports me in every race and it is good to have him there and he loves to be part of it and I am proud to have him with me.'

His mentor, Ron Dennis, was certainly proud of Lewis too: 'His avoidance of debris and restarts were all impeccable. He had a text-book race. He did not put a foot wrong, drove the car faultlessly and did not have one single thing gifted to him. He won the race from start to finish. That makes it special because many drivers win their first and sometimes their only wins from circumstances that are unusual. This was a straight-out, full-on tremendous achievement at one of the most difficult circuits in the world.'

It was, of course, special to Anthony Hamilton but he was keen to analyse how his son kept out of trouble during a chaotic Grand Prix: 'You get all that stuff in karting. It is just a question of keeping your head straight and trying to make a good break. A lot of young guys racing karts dream of being in Formula One and he is really, really enjoying it. I just think it's nice to remain normal and keep your feet on the ground.'

Then there was the perspective on a victory after several second places: 'A sense of relief isn't the right phrase. A sense of relief will come when we retire, I think. It's always going to be exciting. It is always going to be dangerous. I will always have heart palpitations when he is out there driving and I have got another ten or more years of this. I probably feel like everyone else feels. I am just drained. It is fantastic. I can't explain how I feel other than the fact that if you guys feel good then I feel a thousand times better than that.'

Now attention would turn to the United States Grand Prix in Indianapolis the following weekend but not until the normally disciplined young man had a chance to celebrate:

'There's plenty of time to enjoy it before going to Indy and we'll obviously go there with great confidence. I've no doubt that we can do well there.'

One of Lewis's most vocal admirers – former World Champion Niki Lauda – needed no convincing of that: 'The hardest thing is to win your first race and then it is much easier because you have less pressure. You have proved it to yourself.'

Spyker Ferrari's chief technical officer, Mike Gascoyne, who was chief engineer at Renault when Fernando Alonso arrived at the team, was full of praise too: 'The best make it look easy. That's clearly what Lewis is going to be. Now he goes to Indianapolis thinking he is going to win there and why not? McLaren look absolutely dominant.'

However, the nominal team number one had been far from dominant and soon another cloud arrived over the McLaren team when Fernando Alonso voiced his views about life alongside the emerging superstar on a Spanish radio station: 'Right from the start I have never felt totally comfortable. I have a British teammate in a British team. He's doing a great job and we know that all the support and help is going to him. I understood that from the beginning. But I've won two races out of six, I've finished on the podium four times and I have those 40 points that will allow me to fight for the title in the end.'

Ron Dennis was to again assert that neither driver was favoured while allowing for Fernando's orientation in the team: 'There is healthy competition between the teams working on each car – this is inevitable and there is no issue with that. However, I can categorically state once again that both drivers have equal equipment and equal support. Fernando and Lewis know this and support this. Fernando hasn't been with the team long and the relationship can only continue to develop.'

However, it was considered prudent from that point that McLaren's drivers would speak of each other only in each other's company. Ron Dennis explained: 'The consequences just make it more difficult to be what we want to be and that is totally open and cooperative with the media. And now we have a situation where the drivers – who are not controlled by us; we are a team – have to be aware of the fact that it doesn't matter how innocent or well-structured an answer is in respect of a question about their teammate, one in ten will be spun. So they will be more controlled and mindful of anything they say about each other. They have agreed independently of us that they will only talk about each other in each other's presence because then there is no misconception and no misunderstanding.' Also, just in case there was any doubt on the practical side, McLaren's engineering director, Paddy Lowe, explained that within thirty seconds of either car coming to rest in a practice session its driver had his own data sheet, showing every engineering parameter available and an overlay from his teammate's car. They debriefed at the same table, with engineers and strategists from both sides of the garage.

Lewis was briefed about Alonso's outburst shortly before arriving in Indianapolis and had responded: 'I find it strange he said that. I feel ever since he joined the team they have been motivated to push us both towards winning. Ron and the other guys are working hard to make sure we have equal opportunity. Obviously I have a great relationship with the team because I have been there since I was thirteen, but, at the end of the day, when he came to the team everyone was extremely excited. He has a very good relationship with everyone so I don't see why he should say that. Because he is Spanish and I am English I can see how he might feel that but I don't agree with it personally.'

Lewis also agreed that his teammate was possibly startled by his outstanding start in Formula One: 'I doubt he was expecting me to do as well as I am. I don't know if that is why he is saying what he is saying. He is the two-time World Champion. He has never been challenged by someone as closely as me, and by someone who is also a close friend off the track. So it's a very difficult situation.'

Bernie Ecclestone was facing a difficult situation himself as America had been slow to fall for F1's charms: 'The problem is that in the States we don't have that many sponsors; there are no teams and only one driver. There is no mainstream TV coverage and only four races are shown live.' In the absence of a real American focal point around which to build the marketing, Indianapolis was in need of a selling point. Suddenly it had one in the shape of Lewis Hamilton. 'Next Stop for Super-Rookie' exclaimed the banner on the Indianapolis website. The appeal of the young man was irresistible and he could galvanise the neutral like the organisers hoped as they looked at potential walk-up figures.

Of course, so far his only sighting of the circuit had been by electronic means but he would not let that inexperience dampen his spirits: 'I go to Indy with great confidence. It still hasn't really sunk in that I have won my first race – it was an amazing weekend for me and it is fantastic that we are racing again this weekend. The Motor Speedway is another tough circuit on the cars. I've seen the track only on computer games. I don't really know what to expect. I've watched the previous races and onboard footage and looked at data. But I'll be going there with an open mind and having to do the same sort of job I did in Canada.'

Lewis had several promotional engagements before the Grand Prix, one in Manhattan and the other in Washington DC. The Canadian Grand Prix had played out to a packed house. Now Lewis was assisting potential tickets south of the border. His appeal was obvious but with an element of sensitivity. His ethnicity lay at the heart of his draw for so many who were not associated with mainstream motor racing. McLaren baulked at the Tiger Woods reference but though other drivers had achieved much in motor sport, none had been black. Other golfers had won major championships, but none were of Afro-American descent. So it was left to the great man himself to hail Lewis Hamilton as a 'terrific role model'. So proving that six podium finishes in his first six races was making the entire sporting world sit up and notice. The American admirer had almost single-handedly sent golf's popularity soaring since he had turned professional a year ago. As golf's first black superstar, millions of youngsters from minority groups regarded Woods as an inspiration and he felt that Lewis Hamilton would soon have the same appeal. Woods commented: 'I've been following his progress pretty closely and I think it is great that he won the Canadian Grand Prix after going so close in all his previous races. Without a doubt, he is one of the most exciting talents to hit the sporting scene in recent years. Any time that a rookie comes through and wins big, it is a story that captures the imagination. But it's not just his results, I've been impressed by the way he has handled himself off the race track and I think he has the potential to be a terrific role model. I love motor racing. My caddie, Steve Williams, is a speed freak who races back in New Zealand. He got me hooked. I'll be interested to see how Lewis Hamilton goes in the Grand Prix on Sunday and I will catch up with it at some stage.'

When made aware of Tiger Woods' assessment despite his own challenges at the US Open at Oakmont, Lewis was thrilled: 'Now that has put a smile on my face. He's a cool dude and I've always wanted to meet him, so that's nice to hear. Tell him, thank you very much for his kind words. I'm honoured that he's said so many nice things about me and has been taking notice of what I've been doing. I really, really hope to see him soon and I wish him all the best. I know he's going to win, so he doesn't need me to send him any luck.'

Soon it was plain that the Americans had taken to their hearts a good-looking and polite young man with a maturity beyond his twenty-two years, for there was a frenzied reaction when he was introduced to fans at an open question and answer session at the Motor Speedway on the Thursday. He did not disappoint them and Joie Chitwood, the circuit president, was impressed: 'You can just tell he's got that something. If he continues to perform, he's going to be an outstanding ambassador for Formula One.' However, there was suffocating media attention to deal with too. As he chatted with a good friend Robert Kubica, the BMW Sauber driver who had survived a horror smash at the Canadian Grand Prix, so he found himself mobbed by dozens of cameramen. He dealt with this and on arriving at the McLaren Mercedes hospitality area confirmed that he did not find being the centre of attention too much of a problem: 'I'm very, very strong mentally and I can control myself without a problem. That's because I'm not feeling any pressure.'

So to the initial outings on Friday where Lewis would have to get to know the circuit: 'The really tricky bit is the mid-section as it's very tight and twisty. We spent our time fine-tuning the set-up and evaluating the two different tyre options provided by Bridgestone this weekend. In the first part of the second session I ran a little wide and did some minor damage to the aerodynamic fences which took a little time for the guys to repair. We have a pretty good idea of where we are going, and it looks like we should be competitive, but as always Friday is only the start of the weekend – there is a long way to go.'

Quite a way to go but after playing catch-up with teammate Fernando Alonso, Lewis gained the upper hand when it mattered on the Saturday. For he set two laps good enough for pole position and the second of them, at 1:12.331, put him 0.169 ahead and into pole position for the second weekend running. He was more than pleased but expressed some surprise: 'Prior to qualifying I hadn't found an optimal set-up and Fernando looked extremely quick. My two last laps were spot on, though, and I couldn't be happier.' He then paid tribute to the support from the fans: 'I could see a trackside banner with my name on it as I headed back to the pits. The fans have been brilliant to me all weekend and I really appreciate it.'

After an overnight engine change, Lewis knew his latest success was down to total effort: 'Whenever I have gone out I have found extra bits of time. Experience is everything here and the more laps I did the faster I got. The first and last sectors aren't that hard to learn, but initially I was losing about half a second in the middle sector and I have been chipping away at that.' He added interestingly: 'This feels even better than my first pole, in Canada last weekend. During the slowing-down lap I was screaming into my helmet. I felt absolutely thrilled.' Anthony was understandably delighted too: 'Obtaining pole position in Montreal last weekend was one thing, but repeating the feat is more difficult. It's another big hurdle that Lewis has overcome.'

Meanwhile, Fernando Alonso was circumspect after facing another challenge against the persistent rookie: 'I was fastest in every session until the last one. This gives me a lot of confidence. I think I can do really well. I have the pace.'

Not quite enough in the final analysis as Lewis Hamilton continued to turn the pre-season form book on its head with a close-fought victory over his teammate. He secured his second win in as many weeks with a flawless drive from that pole position. When Alonso pulled level with him at 200mph going into the first turn just after half-distance Lewis was not fazed. The novice kept his nerve to make sure the World Champion did not squeeze past. He later admitted that he had had to work very hard during the second stint of the race as Alonso pulled up on to his tail when he was briefly slowed by a lack of grip from his tyres: 'The first couple of laps were close and then I managed to pull a slight gap and maintain it, and in the middle stint my tyres began to grain so Fernando was right up my tail. It was extremely difficult. He was in my slipstream and it was very tough but he fought very well, very professional but in the end I was able to pull a gap, maintain it and win the race.'

Alonso indicated that he had no complaints about the outcome of the race despite waving his fist at the pit crew from the cockpit as the race finished. He was clearly annoyed that the team would not order Hamilton to surrender the lead. However, he concluded: 'It was really close. I think at the start also it was very close but I didn't manage to overtake Lewis then and from then on you follow someone you lose a little bit of downforce and it's difficult to build the tyre's condition during the stint. You maybe damage your tyres more running behind someone. I tried in the middle stint. I was side by side once but it was not enough to overtake him. And the last stint was maybe a conservative one. It was very difficult to overtake.'

As for the victory: 'What a dream,' uttered Lewis, 'to come into two circuits that I didn't know, first time. To really come out with such a pace and see the team moving forward and being competitive. They have done a fantastic job. This wouldn't have been possible without them. I am just extremely pleased and proud of the team. I never thought in a million years I would be here against these drivers. It is a great leap in my career and my life. I am thankful to my family and the guardians of the team.'

For Lewis this was not just his second win by which he led the Championship from Alonso by ten points, it was his seventh podium finish in seven races – an achievement no one had come close to before. He also became the first rookie to win the United States Grand Prix.

Red Bull driver Mark Webber offered an interesting perspective on this stunning start to a Formula One career – that of the new tyres being used this season. The Australian maintained that more experienced drivers had been hampered by adapting to the new Bridgestone control tyres.

'It has been very difficult for the guys who are seasoned campaigners to get used to these tyres,' said Webber. 'The cars are vastly different but that final feel for us in terms of the confidence in the car is the tyres.' Mark described this as one of a 'few little subtleties that have helped Lewis along the way' and stated that many regard tyres as 'boring'. However, he pointed out that the Bridgestones behaved very differently from the Michelin rubber used by many of Hamilton's rivals in previous years. McLaren teammate Fernando Alonso and Ferrari's Kimi Räikkönen had been particularly badly affected because they had driven on Michelins for at least the last five years. 'It's like a golf or tennis player using all the same rackets. Lewis, with his fresh and naïve approach, that's all he knows. Fernando has struggled big time on these tyres. And that's not an excuse and Fernando hasn't used it as one because it's up to us to get on top of it, Kimi is the same. But most of us have found it very frustrating.' Mark Webber did emphasise that he was not diminishing the newcomer's achievements: 'Lewis has unquestionably a huge amount of talent and he has an amazing career ahead of him.'

Meanwhile, it was the moment for two World Champions to add their weight to the speculation that Lewis Hamilton could actually win the Drivers' Championship. Four-time champion Alain Prost believed that Lewis only had himself to beat: 'He's been very impressive. I don't see what can stop him unless it goes to his head.' Prost added: 'I can understand Alonso being upset. He didn't expect to be up against such a promising new driver.' Emerson Fittipaldi – once the youngest champion at twenty-five – was also backing McLaren's twenty-two-year-old to win the title and take the record from Fernando Alonso: 'I would go for Lewis now, for sure. When you are so young and suddenly you are leading and winning, it is a tremendous pressure and he is taking the pressure in a positive way.'

Obviously, Lewis Hamilton was asked for his opinion on his title chances at this stage and, as ever, tried to come up with a balanced view: 'I still approach every race the same as I approached the first. I'm still on a very steep learning curve and there are going to be some negatives this season, some ups and some downs, and I need to be prepared for that. But I am in the best team; I've got the best opportunity to win the title. I've had two wins already and I'm leading the championship by ten points, which is just unreal. So I've just got to enjoy it and we'll see. If I am consistent and keep on producing the same results as I've done so far then I think there is no reason why I wouldn't win the World Championship.'

At this point McLaren made it clear they had no intention of trying to impose any team orders for the rest of the season. 'If that circumstance develops in a manner that goes wrong then I have to get involved, but that is not the case at the moment,' said the team principal Ron Dennis. 'I do not discuss anything with the drivers because I have full commitment from both of them that, as and when appropriate, they discuss it among themselves.

I don't want to know what they said. It is for them to function as teammates.'

Ron was also finding the media rumpus about his drivers' relationship time-consuming and, more importantly: 'Other team principals see it as an opportunity to spring one of the drivers out of the system. At Indianapolis the Italian media started a wave of Alonso–Ferrari stories. When these things happen, innocently or deliberately, they are constructively spoken about. They just don't even get close to smouldering, let alone being a fire.'

When he arrived back home, Lewis began to be aware of the impact he was making on the British sporting scene at both a private and public level. He observed: 'Simple things like going out for dinner, to the cinema or the petrol station are not the same and I get more people coming up to me but I'm trying to keep my feet on the ground. It's strange being described as a celebrity. There are photographers outside my house and that has been the weirdest thing. They're there from eight in the morning until six at night just sitting their cars.'

At the Goodwood Festival of Speed he was asked to stand on a balcony and wave to thousands of cheering fans. They braved atrocious conditions to honour the young man who had put the 'grand' back into Grand Prix. Lewis admitted: 'I stood there in front of all those people. It's incredible, amazing and I'm enjoying it. It's great to see them supporting me. I was surprised.' He added: 'I've been rubbing shoulders with Sir Stirling Moss and Sir Jackie

Stewart – great, amazing people, and they always have good words of wisdom. It's a privilege.'

The West Sussex venue was packed with children eager to see their new hero and he was determined to make time for them – drawing on memories of when he was himself just a kid looking up to the F1 stars. 'When I was just ten and I'd won my first British Championship in karting, I remember going up to drivers for their autograph, but they never looked at me when they signed except for David Coulthard. The rest just brushed past me. So I said that if I ever got to Formula One I'd always look at the kid, or whoever it might be, I'd be signing an autograph for.'

As he contemplated his next big test on track at the French Grand Prix, Lewis revealed to an attentive audience the key to his current situation of two wins in seven races and his consecutive podium finishes: 'Never give up under any circumstances. It doesn't have to be in racing, it can be in anything. When I'm in a race, if I'm at the back or something has gone wrong, I never give up, I keep pushing and it turns good.'

Chapter Seven

AU CONTRAIRE

When Lewis arrived at Magny-Cours his first thought was to look up those who assisted him on the ladder to success, so he sought the paddock set aside for the support races – not the usual territory for the superstars of Formula One.

'That was so typical of Lewis,' reported John Booth of the Manor Motorsport F3 team. 'There he was facing a big weekend, leading the World Drivers' Championship, and he took time to come and have a chat. Lewis has this natural way which gets everyone on side. Ayrton Senna would have the same aim, but be manipulative. When we were racing together, Ayrton was a very pleasant young man but he'd be quite cold about it. He would say: "I will do this, and I will get the mechanics on my side." But with Lewis, you could see him bouncing about with a smile on his face. That's the way he's always been. It's been wonderful to see him maturing. A lot of drivers have promise but not all of them develop and mature. Lewis has done that but the way he has become mistake-free in F1 is the thing that has impressed me most.'

Although the McLaren protégé had swept aside his rivals in the 2006 GP2 series, he had not dominated matters at Magny-Cours. 'It's not been one of my best circuits to race at,' he admitted. 'The French round of the GP2 Championship last season was not my best weekend as I had a coming-together in the first race. That led to my starting race two from nineteenth. I did make my way through the field to fifth to score some points, so it is possible to overtake here. Although you always want to be on pole, you can pass at Magny-Cours, while there is a short pit lane that means there are more strategy options. It is not so much a penalty when you stop for tyres and fuel. At the moment I'm obviously more looking forward to the British Grand Prix at Silverstone because it's my home circuit. But I know I first need to go to Magny-Cours and score points to maintain my lead in the championship. To be going there as championship leader is an awesome feeling. I'm really surprised to see myself with such a gap in the championship and surprised that I've done so well in the last seven Grand Prix. But the key is consistency and I'm working as hard as I can to stay in the zone for the remainder of the season.'

Lewis had followed his appearance at the Goodwood Festival of Speed on the previous Sunday by attending an event in London on the Thursday where he was again given a rousing reception. However, he could not wait to get back to the real business that weekend: 'I just want to get back out on track. But my aims remain the same

– to take it race by race and keep focused on scoring good points for myself and the team.'

His teammate was in a more upbeat mood about the French circuit than perhaps Lewis had been earlier: 'Although they have very different characteristics in general, there are some similarities between Magny-Cours and Monaco. They have a lot of tight, twisty corners, so given the car performed well at Monaco, I am looking forward to getting it out on track in France.'

However, both McLaren drivers were to be somewhat disappointed when Ferrari's Felipe Massa claimed pole position after beating Lewis Hamilton into second in Saturday qualifying. Massa's teammate Kimi Räikkönen was third but Fernando Alonso was struck by mechanical problems and would go off tenth when the race started. The Brazilian clocked 1:15.034, just 0.070 seconds ahead of the Englishman. Massa's pole suggested that Ferrari would become a real threat again at Magny-Cours.

Despite that, Lewis was in an upbeat mood: 'You can't be perfect all the time but the team has done a fantastic job. I had the car for pole but I lost a bit of time at turn fifteen, but I'm very happy. We are on the front row and we've got a good strategy for tomorrow. I'm sure we will be very competitive. Everyone makes improvements and steps forward. Ferrari have done that, but I still believe we have the best car and we just have to prove that tomorrow.'

When it came to the crunch it was Kimi Räikkönen who won the French Grand Prix. He came home two seconds ahead of his teammate Felipe Massa as the Italian team ended McLaren's three-race sequence of victories. Massa, who had led for most of the race, finished ahead of Lewis Hamilton but the rookie extended his lead in the Drivers' Championship to 14 points, with 64 points to 50 over his teammate Fernando Alonso, who was unable to fight through the field and finished seventh. Massa was to be 17 points adrift at this stage and Räikkönen 22 points.

The Ferrari pair made an electric start when the lights went out with Massa pulling clear to lead and Räikkönen outpacing Hamilton to take second place from third on the grid. The McLaren driver chased hard, but though he ran away from Robert Kubica in the BMW Sauber, he could not challenge the two leaders. Massa reeled off a sequence of fastest laps and by the tenth lap he was 3.6 seconds clear of Räikkönen, who was himself 1.7 seconds in front of Hamilton, with Kubica a further 6.9 seconds behind.

Hamilton was the first man into the pits after lap sixteen and was followed seconds later by Alonso. Massa led until the end of lap nineteen when he entered the pits and left Räikkönen to lead for three laps. When the Finn came in, the positions reversed again. Alonso finally passed an obstinate Nick Heidfeld of BMW Sauber on lap thirty-four and three laps later both he and his teammate pitted in succession, as they had done earlier. This left them in third and ninth places again. For Massa and Räikkönen it came down to the second pit stop of the seventy-lap race. Massa led at two-thirds distance on lap forty-three but while his stop took 9 seconds, that of Räikkönen – who came in three laps later – was just 7.8 seconds, allowing him to surprisingly take the lead and the victory.

Lewis was realistic, having lost out at the first corner: 'I don't like to be overtaken. Nobody does. It was the first time. It's inevitable and I'm still on the podium. I think we are the most consistent team and I've extended my lead so I couldn't be happier. You can't win every race. I don't think they were as fast as they looked, but traffic, strategy and being behind them had a lot to do with it. I still think we can take it to them at Silverstone.'

Chapter Eight

HOMECOMING AND HYPE

The week leading up to the British Grand Prix was to provide Lewis with a full diary and some interesting invitations. This led to his being featured in the gossip columns, pictured getting out of a car with pop star Natasha Bedingfield after going out with rapper P Diddy. 'I was invited out to a party by P Diddy on Sunday night but I was tired after the French Grand Prix so I had dinner and went to bed. Then on Monday, I was playing golf in Woking and I got a call saying P Diddy had invited me to a special dinner. I wanted to play the last nine holes so I was seriously contemplating not going. But I got there and they waited for me before they started dinner. Out of all his guests I was sitting next to P Diddy, so I was glad I went. I met a lot of people there. I met the Sugababes and Trevor Nelson. Pharrell Williams had his own Mercedes Vito there and we took that to another place where they were having drinks. Pharrell got out first, I got out second and just being a gentleman I gave her my hand and helped Natasha out of the car. And someone took a picture.'

On Wednesday Lewis was keeping the headline-writers happy again with some interesting comments he made to guests of Tag Heuer, his watch sponsor, at a function. He looked relaxed and composed as he faced an interview with a selected panel including BBC sports presenter Gabby Logan. He answered questions about his attitude in the cockpit, emphasising that he was an attacking driver and liked to take risks. He fielded a reference to his music tastes by confirming his catholic tastes for hip-hop, reggae, house, funky dance music and classical. Then Lewis came out with the declaration: 'I want to spend the rest of my career with McLaren.' This sent the reporters present into a spin and was to create some additional column inches with respect to the response from sports agents too. The twenty-two-year-old said that he was not driven by money and would not be tempted by a lucrative switch to rivals Ferrari. 'I love everyone at the team. I enjoy working with them and I couldn't imagine working anywhere else. If I'm not happy then team boss Ron Dennis and I have to sit down and talk. But that's not the case. I have a great feeling about this team. There is a lot of emotion there because I have grown up with them. Everything is perfect at the factory with the way things are run and the people there.'

Pressed about a potential Ferrari offer, Lewis replied: 'I would not find it difficult to say "no" because I'm not here for the money. It's not something that has driven me to get to Formula One. If Ron Dennis had come up to me last year and said "I'll give you the drive, but you are

Above: 1. Aerial view of Mallory Park, where Lewis Hamilton had his first ever race test in a Formula Renault, aged seventeen.

Right: 2. Lewis with McLaren team owner Ron Dennis in 1997.

3. A curly-haired Lewis on the podium in his GP2 days.

4. With his father Anthony. The two have a strong bond and Anthony has made certain to keep Lewis grounded during his meteoric rise.

5. With Fernando Alonso in happier times prior to the first race of the 2007 season. The relationship between the McLaren teammates would become increasingly fractious as the season wore on.

6. In an F1 car at last: Lewis in qualifying for the Australian Grand Prix.

7. Action from Monaco. The McLarens of Alonso (1) and Hamilton led the field by some distance, but Lewis was advised to maintain the status quo rather than challenging his teammate for first place. Unlike the later espionage scandal, the controversy over these 'team orders' passed fairly quickly.

8. A hand raised in celebration as Lewis Hamilton wins his first Grand Prix in Montreal.

9. Getting a taste for champagne after another win, this time in the United States.

Opposite above: 10. Back in the UK, Lewis goes back to his karting roots, meeting aspiring racers at the Daytona circuit, Milton Keynes.

Opposite below: 11. England expects: with Lewis on pole position at Silverstone, the stage was set for a triumphant homecoming. However, Ferrari's Kimi Räikkönen drove a fantastic race to take the spoils.

12. A sight F1 fans expect to see many times in the coming years: Lewis Hamilton celebrating on the podium after another race win.

not going to be paid" then any driver would have jumped at it. I believe that. Sure, every driver has his value and you want to be respected – and at some point you have to be paid your value – but again, money is not something that drives me. As I've said, I'm really, really happy here.'

Immediately, leading driver managers were warning Lewis Hamilton not to commit his long-term future to the McLaren team who launched him into Formula One. Many believed that Lewis would feel obliged to stay with McLaren as payback for the faith and five million pounds of investment. But experienced managers believed that Anthony Hamilton would make a big mistake if he did not insist on a 'get-out' clause in his son's new contract. The protégé was believed to be earning about £340,000 in his first season with bonuses able to top that up to one million pounds if he became World Champion. However, agents pointed out that McLaren had got their five million back by not employing a more expensive driver. It was also felt that his deal in 2008 could catapult the Stevenage sensation into the big league with a pay packet of £20 million a year. One top manager expressed the opinion that whatever his feelings of loyalty to McLaren, Lewis must keep his options open: 'Things change quickly in Formula One. Look at Jenson Button. He is a great driver who has had no chance of challenging for a championship. Lewis must go where the best car is to keep winning.'

It was also well analysed and publicised that the young man was poised to become Britain's highest paid sportsman according to marketing and sponsorship experts. It was estimated that if he continued to take the chequered flag, Lewis could earn a billion dollars over a ten-year career. That would surpass the 500 million dollars believed to have been earned by multi-World Champion Michael Schumacher over his fifteen years in Formula One.

There was no doubt that by now Lewis Hamilton had transformed a 2007 sporting landscape in which the England football team was not doing well in qualification for Euro 2008; England's cricketers suffered in the Ashes and the World Cup; and only Tim Henman competed and then didn't progress into the second week of the Wimbledon tennis tournament.

ITV executives were beaming at the Hamilton factor and the increase in viewing figures, which had reached 7.7 million in recent weeks. An ITV spokesman commented: 'Lewis Hamilton appeals not just to the core petrol heads but to the average guy on the street. He has attracted a new demographic to the audience because he is young and black.'

Silverstone was a sell-out with 85,000 tickets snapped up. Online retailers had been inundated for Lewis Hamilton merchandise and the betting industry was galvanised by the interest in the British Grand Prix after a busy season. A Ladbroke's spokesman explained: 'Even before Hamilton's first race there was little to suggest a betting boom but his first podium finish saw a huge upsurge. Betting on race two increased by seventy-five per cent across all channels and this year has broken all previous records on turnover.' Bookmakers were anticipating a five million-pound turnover on the race and big payouts if Lewis were to triumph.

There was no lack of support and advice from those interested, with Sir Jackie Stewart commenting: 'If I was to offer him one salient piece of advice – and it is something Lewis has already acknowledged – it would be "don't let it go to your head" but Lewis has the type of head not to be intoxicated by it.' David Coulthard was a shrewd observer of the scene after his many years at the top and had a perspective on the various stages ahead: 'The guys in their first years are so approachable, so nice, still fly Easyjet. Go to the factory, all of those things. When I was a test driver at Williams, I was at the factory every day because frankly, I had nothing else to do. I was trying to soak up as much information as possible and create a career for the future. As Lewis inevitably moves offshore and grows into his life, he will spend less time at the factory because there just won't be the time. He will need energy and recovery time to maintain the level that he's already achieved over the next ten years.'

Less than twelve hours after the London function which was to produce such a reaction, Lewis Hamilton was looking ten years back rather than ten years forward. For, on behalf of Vodafone, the team's main sponsor, he was at a windswept kart track in Milton Keynes to give a pep talk to the top ten drivers in the British Cadet Championship where it had all begun for him.

A multitude of TV crews, photographers and journalists had descended on the Daytona Kart Track and out of a grey Buckinghamshire sky a purple helicopter descended. As Lewis emerged into the paddock area, dressed in his race suit, the air was punctuated with the sound of shouting snappers and camera shutters. The ten Cadet racers and their immediate families were obviously excited that they were about to meet him.

After an introduction and short interview with the ITV F1 host Steve Rider, Lewis climbed into a kart and headed out on to the track for several flying laps. Now togged up in a miniature version of the McLaren suit, the lads, aged eleven to thirteen, gathered around as he dispensed technical tips combined with philosophy, such as: 'It's not just about braking as late as possible – sometimes you need to sacrifice a little bit of entry speed to get a good exit.' As well as: 'You can't just be a racing driver. You have to work hard at school. You have to be able to communicate with people if you want to do the job properly. You need the whole package. And the most important thing of all – never give up.'

Then the ten wannabe Lewis Hamiltons took to the track for a six-lap race and when twelve-year-old Alex Albon crossed the line first, there was a British racing hero waving the chequered flag. His reaction to Alex's performance: 'I'm glad I'm not out there – I'd get my arse kicked!' The presentation of trophies over, Lewis climbed back into the helicopter and flew to Silverstone in preparation for a weekend that fans were also looking forward to. Not before another reminder of his roots as it was announced that a bend was to be named after him at the Rye House nursery track that he had cut his karting teeth on. John Huff, events co-ordinator at the Hoddesdon track in Hertfordshire, was pleased to relate: 'By way of tribute to Lewis's achievements, we have earmarked a part of the circuit which we would like to name Hamilton's. I don't profess to be close mates of the Hamiltons, but I was here when he climbed into his first go-kart and I can remember he was invariably at the front of the grid.' The Rye House Rocket replied: 'This is the environment where I learned my racing craft and what I used to love doing – without it I wouldn't be where I am today.' So Lewis Hamilton showed no sign of forgetting that his new-found fame was the product of his talent at the wheel of a Formula One car.

It had been seven years since David Coulthard had won on home soil but, with no disrespect to the Scottish driver, it was estimated that his victory in 2000 would be nothing to the frenzy that would erupt if Lewis Hamilton took the chequered flag to extend his lead in the drivers' standings.

Lewis made it public that he regarded the forthcoming Sunday as 'the biggest race of the year'. He explained: 'It's my debut home race. It is going to be another new experience, and I expect the atmosphere will be incredible. I cannot wait to race in front of my home fans. To win at this race would be immense, but we have to be realistic with our expectations. This is one race out of seventeen, and as with all the Grand Prix, I will do my best to win for the fans. But the most important thing is for them to enjoy the whole weekend whatever the result will be.'

That the twenty-two-year-old Englishman recorded the fastest time in the first practice session at 1:12.1 seconds at 142mph in a swirling wind didn't surprise anybody, nor did the close performances of Kimi Räikkönen, Felipe Massa and Fernando Alonso in formation behind him. The stage was set for a contest which could even overshadow an espionage row that had broken out between McLaren and Ferrari. Of course, the suggestion that a Ferrari engineer might have been passing secrets to McLaren certainly added extra spice to proceedings. The McLaren boss Ron Dennis insisted that he was not aware of any wrongdoing: 'My integrity is woven into the fabric of the company.' Lewis Hamilton strongly reiterated that fact when questioned by an ever-present media. However, it was understandable that he was keener to comment on track conditions during practice and to laud the qualities of racing at a circuit such as Silverstone: 'I think that out of a lot of the circuits I found that today following another car was similar to the experience I had in GP2. You can actually stay behind them in some of the corners. I don't know if that is because it is so windy here. You maybe slip out of their slipstream and are unable to get plenty of downforce. I think you'll see plenty of overtaking during the race.'

First there was the matter of final qualifying and Lewis was to send Silverstone wild as a dramatic last-lap charge saw him storm to pole position. He scorched round the circuit in 1:19.997 seconds to oust the Ferrari Finn by 0.102 seconds, with McLaren teammate Fernando Alonso third and Ferrari's Felipe Massa fourth. While the fans hailed the first home driver to take that position since Damon Hill in his title-winning year of 1996, his father Anthony was dancing a dance of delight in the pit lane and the rest of the McLaren team hugged each other 'Ferrari and Kimi were extremely quick and it all came down to that last lap when I had to produce a big performance. I'm very excited about tomorrow. I could see so many fans out there today. I came across the line and I could hear the crowd, but I was screaming as loud as them. I nearly lost my voice.'

His father declared: 'I always think he has got a chance and I always thought he was going to do it but I was worried when I saw the time ticking down. But I knew it couldn't be that bad. He was just waiting I am sure, and he flew through the last two sectors. In Karting you can do that last-lap dash. He is familiar with doing that, Lewis, coming from nowhere and sticking it on pole.' Anthony added: 'I don't think the pressure will have got to him. He was digging in, but I don't think there was any extra pressure from the crowd. He wanted to deliver for himself at home. I don't think the pressure of being at Silverstone changed his preparation. He just wants to win.'

Lewis's grandfather, Davidson, had flown over from Grenada to watch him but there was less certainty about his attendance at Silverstone: 'He is seventy-eight and I'm not sure that he can deal with the noise. He may go and watch it round my sister's house and meet up after the race.'

Meanwhile, the pole-sitter admitted that the fact this was his home Grand Prix made the race the most challenging of the season so far: 'No race is easy, of course, but this one is the most challenging, especially in terms of the attention. I hope I can turn it to my advantage. I remember last year, when I won the GP2 races, especially the second race when I went from eighth to first. It was one of my best weekends in the sport and I definitely felt the crowd with me then. I hope the same can happen in the British Grand Prix.'

Kimi Räikkönen, victorious in the previous weekend's French Grand Prix at Magny-Cours, wasn't too impressed with himself: 'I'm disappointed, but hopefully I can make a good start tomorrow. It was going well but I ran off at the last corner.'

So to 1p.m. on the Sunday afternoon and once the five lights disappeared there was no repeat of Lewis's poor start in France. This time around the Briton was clean away, cutting from left to right across the track to defend the inside line heading into the first corner at Copse. It was perfect, but at no stage over the following sixteen laps was he able to get away from Räikkönen, who remained within a second and paying close attention. At one stage the Ferrari driver came alongside his McLaren rival, whose first stop two laps later did not go to plan. Lewis went to pull away as the lollipop man flicked the sign telling him to engage first gear, despite the fact that the car was still being refuelled. With a clear track Räikkönen accelerated further and it proved crucial as the Finn emerged from the pit lane ahead of Hamilton. The leading duo were hotly pursued by Alonso. When the Spaniard pitted on lap twenty for a 6.3-second stop, it allowed him to emerge in the lead with Räikkönen and Hamilton in his mirrors. At that point a home win disappeared for the British McLaren driver as he dropped further and further behind Alonso.

It then became a battle between Alonso and Räikkönen, who held a gap of around five seconds to the World Champion throughout the middle stint until the second round of pit stops. Kimi stayed out six laps longer than Fernando. This was the second turning point of the race as the Ferrari racer reversed the positions and took victory eventually by 2.4 seconds.

Third-placed Lewis still held a 12-point lead over Alonso with Räikkönen's victory moving him into third place, one point ahead of teammate Felipe Massa but still 18 points shy of Hamilton.

'We had a good car all weekend,' said the victor. 'At the beginning I tried to save some fuel and look after the car and tyres. Once we knew we had enough fuel I was able to close on Lewis and try to overtake him. But we knew that he was coming in so didn't take too much of a risk. It was a very nice feeling to win the race. Hopefully, the championship is not over. It's still going to be a long season. We seem to have good speed now but I think it also depends on the circuit conditions at the places we go.'

Lewis claimed that a lack of speed had denied him the chance of victory in his home Grand Prix. 'We had an interesting race. It started off quite well. I was trying to open a gap to Kimi but obviously he was very quick, and at the end of the stint the tyres were starting to fall away. All weekend I was struggling to balance the car. In the last stint it was better. I was very consistent but I just didn't have the pace.'

Many were curious how he would clear his mind and prepare quietly for the next race. Certainly, having survived the pressure of a Silverstone awash with patriotism, the rest of the season would take care of itself. 'When I finish at the track, I go to my parents' home and play golf with my Dad. Then again, golf's no help at all – I'm terrible. I've got a lot of talent for any sport. I can hit the ball, but I'm very inconsistent. My Uncle Terry tells me what to do, but I'm a terrible pupil. I'd take lessons from Tiger however!'

Chapter Nine

DOWN TO EARTH WITH A BUMP

The team had promised Lewis a speedier car for the European Grand Prix at the Nurburgring in Germany. On the initial runs that promise looked fulfilled. Despite suffering from the lingering effects of 'flu, the McLaren number two rose to the challenge to set the fastest time in the morning practice session. In the afternoon only Kimi Räikkönen outpaced him with just five minutes remaining. The gap between the Ferrari and the McLaren was 0.139 seconds – encouraging after a day of changing conditions on track and in the weather conditions. In the earlier session, Lewis had lapped in 1:32.515, Kimi in 1:32.751. Then the rain came down during the lunch break and washed away the rubber that had been laid down. So the second session was slower because of the lower level of grip and the fact that the circuit still had wet patches. Lewis's best was 1:33.478 to Kimi's 1:33.339.

The British driver's summary: 'As always we focused on tyre evaluation and general set-up work. Obviously this was affected a bit by the wet weather. However, I found a good balance early on and I am generally happy with the car. We have introduced some aerodynamic changes this weekend which so far seem to be working well and I know the team has worked really hard since Silverstone. As I haven't run recently on a drying track I went out to gain some more experience, just in case we need it this weekend.' There were two minor errors to note as he had spun in turn ten and later ran wide into the gravel in turn five.

When facing the press in advance of qualifying, there was much discussion with Lewis about his lead in the Drivers' World Championship: 'I'm just happy with the job I've done so far. Anything from here on is a bonus. I'm still going through the season not expecting to win the World Championship. If I don't then that is racing and it was to be expected coming into the season. I've not come into the season saying "I really hope this is my time that I win the World Championship." I didn't build myself up and build my hopes up. If we win – fantastic. It's great for the team, great for me and my career, which of course is what we are working towards. If not, then we just hope for the best. If we continue as we are we should be in the top three.'

The young Briton also conceded that his tactics were changing from an all-out thrust for victory to protecting the existing 12-point lead over teammate Fernando Alonso: 'You drive so close to the edge at the first few races you could easily come off. I am not going to take that risk now and lose points for me and the team. It is no longer about trying to win it at the first corner or desperately turning third into second place. If it is possible to win I will take it but otherwise we will take the points.'

As black clouds rolled off the Eiffel Mountains, it was the World Champion who believed that his greater experience would count in difficult conditions and as the season progressed: 'There are many races to go but experience will help at the end of the championship. Sooner or later there will be difficult weekends, maybe this one. Maybe it rains all weekend. There are many opportunities to lose a race and not so many to win one. You can be lucky or unlucky over a few races but over 17 it is the best who will win, so I am confident.'

How prophetic Fernando proved to be, for the next day his teammate was involved in a heavy crash. The accident happened with just over five minutes of the final qualifying session remaining. Lewis had just made a pit stop to have his final set of tyres fitted and had completed his subsequent out-lap. In the first sector he set what was, at that point, the fastest time. As he accelerated towards turn eight, which is taken at around 160mph, the front-right tyre appeared to fail even before he attempted to turn in. The McLaren bounced over the gravel trap and impacted at over 60mph into the tyre wall. The onboard camera showed Lewis immediately kicking his legs before extracting himself partly from the car to a standing position within the cockpit. He was then assisted by medics and appeared to be winded as he first sat and then lay by the side of the track. The team boss immediately left the pit-lane wall as a stretcher was called for. The

McLaren protégé, wearing an oxygen mask and with a drip applied, waved and gave a thumbs-up sign as he was taken to a waiting ambulance. The session was red-flagged as the young racer was taken to the medical centre. The trackside marshals required time to conduct repairs to the tyre barrier before the session could restart.

Soon team boss Ron Dennis was able to confirm that Lewis had not been seriously injured in the crash, but insisted it was too early to say whether he would be able to participate in the Grand Prix. 'They are keeping him in for a couple of hours' observation but the early indication is that he has no injuries. It's far too early to say but at the moment he doesn't appear to have pain anywhere, no broken bones. We won't be able to decide until after a few hours' observation, but so far, so good.' The McLaren principal then revealed that the smash was caused by 'a failure of the right-hand wheel gun, so effectively the wheel wasn't properly put on.' He added: 'But that's not the mechanic's fault. In fact it was quite fortunate because the same gun was used on Fernando's car and he hadn't started to lean on it yet. We could tell that it was a gun failure. At least we know we don't have a problem with the car.'

If fit to race, Lewis would start from tenth on the grid. Ahead would be Kimi Räikkönen on pole, aiming for a hat-trick of successive victories. Fernando Alonso was also on the front row, but only after almost losing his McLaren in the middle sector on his charging last lap. Fernando had split the Ferraris, with Felipe Massa starting from third.

Eventually it was announced that Lewis had been ᴠ
to take his place in the line-up and he was able to give
insight into his crash: 'It caught me off guard. The lap was
going really well and, all of a sudden, I went up to turn
eight and something just happened. I lost grip and went
straight on. At that point you're just a passenger, so you hold
on for dear life and when you hit the wall, you hope it's
not painful. But it was very painful in my chest and legs. I
waited for a while before I got out of the car. Eventually
I was able to climb out but then I had problems with my
legs. I think that with the shock I couldn't stand up. I was
conscious. I was just in pain in my chest and I had this big
bruise. Thanks to the medical team for doing such a good
job.' He continued: 'I wanted to race. Even when I got
out, I was asking the medical team: "How badly damaged
is my car?"'

Race day itself proved to be problematic for the rookie.
His World Championship lead was eroded to two points
when Fernando Alonso gained an outstanding victory from
Ferrari. In terrible conditions, the Spaniard's third win of
the season put him right back into contention to retain
his title.

Rain had been expected early in the proceedings but
not as soon as the monsoon that turned the track into a
skating rink on the opening lap. From pole position Kimi
Räikkönen took the lead with his teammate Felipe Massa
overtaking Fernando Alonso for second. From tenth Lewis
Hamilton came through to sixth going into the first corner

and fourth by the second, only to slow suddenly with a puncture that would impact negatively on his afternoon.

By now there was torrential rain and the track was awash. The Finn at the front led everybody towards the pits but slid over the slippery pit-lane entry road and back onto the main straight. He now had to crawl around for a further lap before switching to rain tyres. So now Massa led Alonso. It was Jenson Button of Honda who was in pursuit as they went into the first corner for the second time. Then Jenson went off into the tyre wall and within moments his car was joined by the Spyker of Adrian Sutil, the Toro Rossos of Tony Liuzzi and Scott Speed, plus, significantly, the McLaren of one Lewis Hamilton. He was to be the only one who was able to keep his engine running and be lifted back onto the circuit.

Soon conditions were so bad that the officials red-flagged the race, resuming when matters improved, behind the safety car. In a gamble on conditions improving further, Lewis pitted again for dry tyres on the seventh lap. However, it was too soon and he lost ground when he came off the road for a brief time.

When the racing started again on lap eight, Massa and Alonso soon passed temporary leader Markus Winkelhock of Spyker. Another frantic session of pit stops, with drivers switching from intermediate tyres to dry tyres as conditions improved, put Räikkönen back in the frame as he was in third place by lap fourteen. Eventually his challenge came to a halt on lap thirty-five with a hydraulic fault on his

Ferrari. Meanwhile, Massa maintained a lead over Alonso and on lap fifty-three they came into the pits together as the rain came back. Later the Brazilian was to refer to his set of wet-weather tyres vibrating badly, and Alonso did catch him and pass him on the fifty-sixth lap after some wheel-banging incidents. Massa hung on for second place with Mark Webber claiming the final podium place for Red Bull.

The stunning victory by Fernando Alonso sparked an expletive-laden row with the runner-up. The Spaniard stepped out of the car and immediately blamed the Brazilian for their coming-together when the overtaking move was underway in turn four. They were reported as having squared up in the corridor leading to the podium, with Alonso accusing Massa when he said: 'You did that on purpose.' Massa replied: 'You have got to learn to f—ing drive.' Alonso later apologised for his accusation and saw issues in perspective: 'The most important victories are when the main opposition are not in the points. I'm happy for this win, but it is also ten points over Kimi Räikkönen and Lewis, and two over Felipe. So I'm happy for that. There is a long way to go and I will give it my maximum.'

As for the hard-pressed Lewis Hamilton – following his earlier collection of incidents – he swapped fastest laps with Felipe Massa as he climbed steadily towards the points. He had reached eighth position by lap fifty-three until the need to pit for wet tyres dropped him back behind the Renaults. Back on track, Lewis tagged Giancarlo Fisichella but only just failed to catch his Renault teammate Heikki Kovalainen by the flag and so missed out on the final championship point. So the young Briton had battled for sixty laps from 85 seconds down on the leaders to miss out on eighth place by 1.5 seconds.

'This was an extraordinary weekend and a new experience for me,' Lewis explained. 'I made a good start and was sixth then fourth when the two BMWs went off. Then I picked up a puncture. The team took advantage of this and fitted rain tyres but it just got too slippery and I went off. I managed to keep the engine running and a crane was able to get me free – thank you, Nurburgring marshals. After the restart I pushed as much as I could to catch up but when you are almost a lap down you really have to rely on other people's misfortune. I was able to get ninth in the end, but no points.'

Winner Fernando Alonso, who had reduced the Hamilton lead to a slender two points, felt that his teammate's setback was a blip rather than the end of the story. He stated: 'I couldn't put my money on any driver for the last seven races. They are all unpredictable races.'

The Stevenage flyer kept a positive view in the face of adversity: 'I still lead the World Championship and find that quite amusing after everything that has happened. If I was honest I would admit that I had more fun today than in the last nine races. I came here feeling completely sick, had one of the biggest crashes I've ever had, a puncture and even went into the gravel. But it was a great weekend for learning and I learned ten times as much as any other race. You can't have perfect weekends race after race. You have to have different experiences. Today was a new experience with rain, aquaplaning off and deciding whether I used slick or wet tyres. I enjoyed it. Okay, my run of podium finishes has gone but I knew it would and I was ready for that. I hope this is all the bad luck out of the way.'

Many pundits felt it was a tribute to Lewis's tenacity that, even while running last in the queue during the early stages of the race, he got his head down and recorded a succession of fastest laps which inched him towards the pack. And when he was lapped by the front-running contenders he strained every sinew to keep up with them as long as possible. In the eyes of most the young Briton had passed a stern test of his resilience and strength of character.

So Lewis would also head for Hungary the next week a wiser man and tougher opponent. He might not rush so quickly next time to the dry tyres that cost him as the track was drying. He might insist on coming in immediately behind his teammate instead of staying out an extra lap when the rain starts to fall. At the highest level in this sport it could be the small details that made an extra difference. Alonso had been faultless this time. Come Hungary, so might his junior partner.

Previously there had been speculation that Lewis Hamilton would be free to leave McLaren Mercedes should the team be found guilty of pit-lane espionage at a motor racing court hearing in Paris. It was understood that his deal with McLaren, like that of Fernando Alonso, contained a clause which allowed him to move to a rival should his image be damaged by proven malpractice.

The potential loss of Britain's Formula One sensation and the World Champion added extra pressure on Ron Dennis as he defended his company against the charge that they had illegal possession of a 780-page dossier of Ferrari secrets. If found guilty, the punishments McLaren could face ranged from a heavy fine to being docked points, and even being removed from the championships. After ten rounds, McLaren headed Ferrari by 27 points in the Constructors' Championship while Hamilton led Alonso by those two points in the Drivers' Championship. The dilemma confronting the sport was that throwing Lewis Hamilton and Fernando Alonso out of the championship would damage its image and be unfair to those who were not involved.

Eventually, Lewis's place in the World Championship was maintained as McLaren escaped punishment. The FIA's statement, following six hours of deliberations in the Place de la Concorde, said: 'The World Motor Sport Council are satisfied that Vodafone McLaren Mercedes were in possession of confidential Ferrari information and therefore in breach of article 151c of the International Sporting Code. However, there is insufficient evidence that this information was used in such a way to interfere improperly with the FIA Formula One World Championship. We therefore impose no penalty.'

A cloud continued to hang over McLaren, however, because the council reserved the right to exclude them from the 2007 or 2008 seasons if it transpired that they had benefited from the dossier.

The FIA would now focus their attention on Mike Coughlan, McLaren's suspended chief designer who received the documents, and Nigel Stepney, the sacked Ferrari chief mechanic who supplied them.

Meanwhile, the Ferrari team were on the attack: 'Ferrari notes that Vodafone McLaren Mercedes has been found guilty by the FIA World Council. It therefore finds it incomprehensible that violating the fundamental principles of sporting honesty does not have, as a logical and inevitable consequence, the application of a sanction. Today's decision legitimises dishonest behaviour in Formula One and sets a very serious precedent.'

It was obvious at this point that Ferrari would not let the matter rest and that more distracting controversy would swirl around the heads of Lewis Hamilton and Fernando Alonso as they prepared for future races. The Italian team continued: 'The fact that McLaren Mercedes were in possession of such information was discovered totally by accident and, but for this, the team would continue to have it. This is all the more serious as it has occurred in a sport like Formula One in which small details make all the difference. Ferrari feel this is highly prejudicial to the credibility of the sport. So Ferrari will continue with the legal action under way within the Italian criminal justice system, and in the civil court in England.'

Ferrari, who discovered the documents through a tip-off from a Surrey shop assistant who helped Mike Coughlan's wife Trudy copy the dossier, indicated they would fight the matter to a bitter conclusion if they finished the year without the title. They claimed that missing out would cost them four million pounds.

It seemed to many observers that McLaren's immediate escape from punishment would stimulate Ferrari to dig away for more evidence and create an even more poisonous rivalry between the teams that Messrs Alonso, Hamilton, Räikkönen and Massa did not want to get involved in.

Ron Dennis had arrived in Paris declaring 'I'm here for the truth' and was relieved at the outcome, though 'not totally comfortable with it'. Dismissing the offence as a 'technical breach', Ron continued: 'There is no doubt the past twenty-four days have been challenging. Moving forward, McLaren want to reaffirm our longstanding commitment to honesty and integrity, and restate that we believe we have acted correctly throughout. Now we have a Formula One World Championship to win. As a result, we intend to move on, so as to maintain the focus and commitment required to do exactly that.'

Lewis Hamilton welcomed the ruling: 'While it's only my first season in Formula One with the team, I already know and appreciate the commitment and dedication of the people there. As a result, I am pleased with today's decision and can't wait for the rest of the season.'

Chapter Ten

ANYTHING YOU CAN DO...

Espionage was pushed down the Formula One agenda as the key rivals returned to the track in a compelling title tilt at the Hungaroring, a circuit which, like Monaco, placed an emphasis on qualifying. Any hope that rain might allow a race result like that of Jenson Button the previous year disappeared. Not even a shower was forecast.

Fernando Alonso and Lewis Hamilton were closely matched throughout free practice with the Spaniard topping the time sheets in both sessions. For the Briton this was a critical phase of the season with three experienced drivers in hot pursuit knowing the demands of the climax of the season. Nor were Alonso, Räikkönen and Massa at odds with their machines at this point of the season.

Despite ending the afternoon in a gravel trap, Lewis was circumspect in his analysis: 'I've always seen myself as the rookie of the championship, and I'm learning all the way,' he began. 'I'm leading the World Championship, but I don't feel there is too much pressure. I have Fernando breathing heavily down my neck, but that is not too much of a worry. I think I have as good a chance as anyone. I came away from the last race with a smile on my face. Yes, I lost ten points, but I learned so much. I also reminded myself in the race that you never give up.'

The young man's mental strength was about to be severely tested when the qualifying session on the Saturday ended in a furore. Lewis seemed on course to secure his fourth pole position of the season when a pit-lane incident with his teammate cost him a final qualifying lap. The Englishman was obliged to wait in the pit for ten seconds while Fernando Alonso sat in front of the McLaren garage, even though his car was ready to go. The World Champion then set off just in time to start a final qualifying run with precisely one second to spare. Alonso lapped in 1:19.674, which was 0.107 seconds quicker than Hamilton's previous best. That initially gave Alonso pole position until race stewards subsequently decreed that he had unnecessarily impeded his teammate. In the official statement, the actions were deemed to be 'prejudicial to the interests of the competition and motorsport generally'. The Spaniard was punished for his dubious tactic as the stewards moved him back five places and shuffled Lewis Hamilton into pole position. McLaren were also told that their constructors' points would not stand.

McLaren then sought to pour oil on troubled waters with a communiqué pointing out how difficult it was managing two such outstanding drivers in one team, particularly in a winning car: 'Every effort was made yesterday to maintain our policy of equality. We do not believe that the findings of the stewards and the severe penalty imposed on the team are appropriate and that our strenuous efforts to maintain the spirit of fair play and equality within the team have been understood.'

As a result of this decision, David Coulthard joined the fray and called for more consistency when applying penalties in the sport. Fernando Alonso had already criticised the penalty, saying that there was no rule that specified he should be punished in such a situation. Coulthard admitted he was also left wondering why the race stewards decided on that penalty: 'Like many others in the pit lane I am first and foremost a fan of the sport, so I was just as fascinated by the developing rivalry between Alonso and Hamilton after qualifying in Hungary. But a number of us inside F1 circles were also left wondering how the stewards came to decide on the punishment meted out to Alonso and McLaren. Why, for instance was McLaren singled out for punishment while Ferrari wasn't pulled up for failing to put fuel in Felipe Massa's Ferrari? Didn't that hamper Felipe's chances in qualifying as well? It's a bit difficult to follow the sport when you find there isn't really a consistent set of criteria for how penalties are applied.'

This verdict came over eight hours after the conclusion of the qualifying session, by which time many verbal blows were being traded in the McLaren camp. Lewis wanted to know why McLaren held Fernando for so long: 'We sometimes wait a few seconds to make sure we get a clear track but not if it means delaying your teammate.' Fernando took a contrary view: 'We have to wait for the right moment.

That might be five, ten or even forty-five seconds. I was sitting there listening to my engineer's countdown. It's the same at every race.'

Team boss Ron Dennis was visibly angry after the session and was seen on television throwing his headphones when Lewis Hamilton failed to reach the finish line in time to complete his lap. Fernando Alonso told reporters that his teammate had not respected orders from the team to allow him through earlier in the session to enable him to have an extra flying lap: 'They told Hamilton what to do and he didn't listen. That was the only problem the team had. Ron's anger was because he didn't accept an order that the team repeated several times over the first lap. Therefore the team did all they had to do, and tried to give me that extra lap, but for those reasons it wasn't possible.'

Ron Dennis certainly felt that Lewis was partly to blame for the muddle: 'We have to wait for the cars to reach operating temperature before we send them down the pit lane ahead of the final part of qualifying. It was Fernando's turn to go first and get the benefit of a clear track during the fuel burn-off, but Lewis's car was ready earlier. We sent him on his way, but he was supposed to let Fernando by and didn't. That was disappointing.'

Lewis acknowledged his disobedience: 'If I'd let Fernando through there was a danger that Kimi Räikkönen might pass me, too. I didn't want to waste an opportunity that had been presented to me – I took a selfish decision but didn't do anything to impede my teammate.'

Ron Dennis and his protégé exchanged harsh words over the radio after the initial incident. The team boss admitted: 'We were firm with each other but going into details serves no function.' He continued: 'Now, as you have often asked the question, and let me make it a very honest answer, it is extremely difficult to deal with two such competitive drivers. There are definite pressures within the team. We make no secret of it. They are both very competitive and they both want to win. We are trying our very best to balance those pressures. Today we were part of a process where it didn't work and the end result is more pressure on the team. But what you hear is the exact truth of what happened and we will manage it inside the team through the balance of the season.

'Obviously Lewis feels more uncomfortable with the situation than Fernando. That's life, that's the way it is, and if he feels too hot to talk about it then that's the way it is. It's just pressure, competitiveness, and that's the way it is. We've just got to get on and deal with it, but we're not hiding from it.

'We're sat on the front row of the most difficult Grand Prix to win as regards overtaking, and therefore we want to get on with the race.'

Lewis had made the attempt to clear the air with the McLaren principal after their exchange: 'I've been working with Ron for nearly ten years now, so what happened is quite a big event and a problem for the team. Ron was not happy. But we sat down, we spoke about it and he told me that he respected that it was part of my personality. We were professionals so came to a mutual understanding and started with a clean slate. After the argument I had with Ron on the radio, he was angry. I just thought he was teaching me a lesson. I did not think Fernando would do that sort of thing, but I have reasons to believe that this is not the case.'

Obviously the media were keen to find out whether Lewis's respect for Fernando Alonso had diminished after the incident. He was straightforward in his response: 'I wouldn't say it's diminished. I still respect him because coming into F1 I have always been looking to the World Champions and people that have done it and are doing what I want to do. I'm sitting next to a two-times World Champion so I admire him for what he has done.

'I don't particularly think he has a great excuse for what happened today and that tends to lead to certain things. But I just have to let it go over my head, I've got a race to do tomorrow.'

The pair had recently made an 'Anything you can do, I can do better' themed television commercial in which they were featured trying to be first to book into a hotel, competing on an exercise bike and seeing who could withstand the most heat in a sauna: 'We went away on this filming and we really had some fun. We were laughing and joking all the time and it turned out really good. It's pretty cool – anything you can do I can do better! That's a bit like how it is in the team,' Lewis confirmed.

The personal result of the brouhaha for Lewis was that he would now be spared second place on the grid. The Hungaroring lay in a dusty bowl and conditions off the racing line were dirty. At the start of the GP2 race on the Saturday, Andreas Zuber had started from the inside of the front row and was fifth by the first corner. Lewis would line up alongside the BMW of Nick Heidfeld. The German team had efficient software that propelled its cars off the line, but Alonso's penalty meant that Heidfeld inherited Hamilton's original slot on the dirty side of the track.

Lewis insisted that the swirling controversies would not affect his approach: 'Blanking out the other stuff is a skill I have learned over the years. I love my job. It is something I always wanted to do and I still enjoy it. I always have a smile on my face when I get in the car, so it's easy for me to overcome any problems I have in the team and get on with things in the best way I can.'

There were varied views amongst the leading drivers about the choice of tyres. Alonso had initially qualified on pole using the soft-compound tyre. Hamilton, however, chose the super-soft, while Heidfeld did at first but then had a change of mind: 'Tyre choice has been particularly difficult this weekend but I think the harder option will be fine for the race.'

In the final analysis it was Kimi Räikkönen and not Nick Heidfeld who took the battle to Lewis Hamilton in the Grand Prix. From pole position Lewis was able to accelerate cleanly into the lead going into the first corner, swinging across the nose of Nick Heidfeld's BMW Sauber as Kimi Räikkönen came charging through from the second row to relegate the German driver to third place as they exited the first turn. From that time the British leader was never headed. After seventy laps and 306 kilometres, he won by 0.7 seconds ahead of Kimi Räikkönen of Ferrari. Lewis came in on lap nineteen for 9.7 seconds and lap fifty for 4.9 seconds. Fernando Alonso finished fourth. This meant that Lewis led the Drivers' Championship with 80 points from Fernando Alonso in second place on 73 points. Despite the penalty, McLaren Mercedes were still ahead in the Constructor's Championship with 138 points to 119 points, subject to appeal. This was the team's fiftieth victory since the beginning of the partnership between Mercedes-Benz and McLaren back in 1995.

Commented the victor: 'It was a very emotional race and an eventful weekend. During the past two weeks the team has done a great job with the car and we have definitely made a step forward. However, the Ferrari was also as fast today and during the final laps Kimi put a lot of pressure on me. I managed to pull out a slight gap in the first stint but during the last two stints I had some slight problems with the steering of the car. This meant that Kimi was able to close on me which made me a little nervous. But the team told me on the radio that all was well, which meant I could push right to the end.'

Behind Heidfeld, Fernando Alonso was satisfied with fourth: 'We knew it's very hard to overtake at this circuit.

We know it's hard starting from behind but we were dreaming about reaching the podium. We were close but it wasn't enough. But fourth place is not bad. I lost one point compared to the maximum that was possible for us. I spent the whole race in traffic, first with Ralf Schumacher and then with Heidfeld, and it was pretty hard to drive with someone in front.'

Lewis Hamilton's teammate obviously had a view on the impact of the steward's judgement: 'It was a stupid decision but one of those strange things that happen. The race result was determined by last night's decision. This is like when an unfair penalty is called against you in football. You have to keep playing the game with a goal against you.' Alonso added: 'It's a lost opportunity because I think this weekend I was faster. Yesterday I got pole and today when I was in clean air I was very fast so I think I could have won, but it was not to be. In three weeks there's another race and I will try again.' The McLaren number one was still confident that the title battle was not over: 'I think it's not going to be decided until the last race. I was two points behind and now I'm seven behind but we were 14 behind a few races ago so we are doing fine.'

Kimi Räikkönen also insisted he was not giving up on the championship despite his 20-point gap to McLaren rival Lewis Hamilton: 'The championship is not over yet, that's for sure. The gap to the leader has not changed substantially and we can't give up. We have an excellent car and I think the Hungaroring was the only race track so far where we could have expected to have a slight disadvantage compared to McLaren. Whenever we have won a race, as in Magny-Cours and at Silverstone, we made up ground. I'm convinced that when we go back onto a similar track, we can be much more competitive. At Istanbul, Monza and Spa-Francorchamps, where there are many long straights and fast corners, we should be able to play out the F2007's characteristics.'

The Finn indicated his displeasure with the result in Hungary, especially as he believed that he had the pace to beat Lewis Hamilton: 'If there was one driver who should not have been in front of me it was Hamilton. I raced the whole race on second position behind the British driver. I had a really good race rhythm and a good pace. If I had a free track, I could have been much stronger. Before the last lap I slowed down a bit to build up some space ahead of me for a hot lap, just to see what time I could have done. We got the confirmation that we could have gone faster.' The Ferrari driver conceded: 'Hamilton is a really good driver and he did not commit one error. I was looking for a chance behind him and he didn't make any mistake, so I didn't have a possibility to pass him.'

With the result logged, attention moved back to the speculation that one of the most potent driver partnerships in Formula One history was fragile. Lewis Hamilton, who had sparked Fernando Alonso's anger, apologised to his team for his role in the problems but revealed that his teammate was not on speaking terms with him. 'I went round to the whole team and said: "Come on, let's do this, good luck." There was only one person I didn't. That didn't affect me. I got on and did my job. Fernando doesn't seem to have been speaking to me since yesterday, so I don't know if that is a problem. I'm easy to get on with. I don't hold grudges over anyone. If he doesn't want to speak to me, then that's for him to decide. If I see him, I will talk to him but I will not go over and make him feel better. Going into the race there was a big cloud over my mind and it was difficult to stay focused because the team were not getting points. So you didn't know if they hated you or the situation, or who they blamed. I have spoken to them and apologised, but that's the way it is.'

Meanwhile, Ron Dennis was admitting that he was too emotionally drained to be able to enjoy Lewis's dominant win. A downbeat Dennis, when asked how he felt, informed ITV Sport: 'A bit of emptiness at the end of an extremely difficult weekend. I am so drained, it's difficult to have any emotion left. What happened yesterday was really unacceptable. We have a very, very strong commitment to parity. But this was one of those times where as hard as you try, there's always a deviation from our plans – that put the team in an extremely difficult position.' He also emphasised that both drivers were to blame for the mess: 'I don't think either driver is blameless in this situation. We should have been a little more aggressive in handling this situation, but it's not really my style.' He added: 'In the end we are still leading both championships. We have taken a difficult emotional blow but we just have to dig deep and move forward.'

Lewis Hamilton did appreciate that his battle with Fernando Alonso was not helpful to the McLaren cause: 'When you have two very competitive people in a team, probably the two most competitive people around, and who both want to win, it puts the team under pressure. It's just extremely hard for everyone to play fair and make it easy. That's why sometimes it appears one driver is favoured over the other. That's why sometimes I feel he is favoured and vice versa. Because of the problems we are having with the FIA and Ferrari, it's even more pressure on the team.' However, he did offer this insight into McLaren Mercedes: 'The comforting thing is we have all this stuff going on, even at the weekend, and yet we weren't distracted from our job. I learned a lot from the weekend about my team, how strong they are to deal with all the issues that are going on right now. It's daunting for all of us but I don't believe that any team could cope with it better. We thought after the first problem everything would be clear and we could move on, but it's gone way back into it. It's a tough time for the whole team, but it's not distracting us, which is the main thing.'

For Fernando Alonso there were further opportunities taken to offer his perspective on events. He stated that he was stunned by his teammate's outburst at Ron Dennis after final qualifying at the Hungarian Grand Prix: 'I suppose the team will look at it. It is the first time Hamilton, or any driver, speaks like that to his boss. I have never seen it. I suppose they will talk to him and in Turkey things will be back to normal in three weeks. I don't think anything will change in the team.'

It had also been alleged that the Hamilton family instigated the complaint to the stewards – an accusation Lewis denied. The incident had also resulted in the team not receiving the 15 points which would have accrued from the victory and the fourth place for the Constructor's Championship. Speaking on Cadenasur, a Spanish radio station, Alonso said: 'There have been some strange situations in the team all through the year and this was another example. We were first and second in qualifying and nobody was happy. We went to complain about ourselves. It was one of the most surreal moments I have experienced in F1.'

The double champion rebutted suggestions that Formula One's governing body, the FIA, was conspiring to help Lewis Hamilton: 'Everybody asks me that, fans and journalists, but no, I don't think so. It is difficult to organise things to make a driver win with all of the things that can happen in a race, the small details which can make the difference. That is impossible to control.' He refused to confirm if he would see out his contract with McLaren which had a further two years to run after the 2007 season. When quizzed on the matter by Spanish journalists, he replied: 'I don't know, I don't know.'

By now Formula One was in possession of one of the most intriguing and extraordinary stories in sport, and it was headline news across the globe. In Spain it was inevitable that Lewis Hamilton would be cast as the villain. To quote *El Pais* on the pit-lane confrontation between Hamilton and Alonso: 'It was an intolerable dialogue for Dennis, who must worry about maintaining the sport's pure image. The damage that Hamilton has inflicted on the team is terrible, as is the disillusionment he has caused in a man who has given him his all. With the intervention of the sport's commissioners, prompted by Hamilton's father, Hamilton held on to pole position while Alonso was relegated to sixth place.' The article continued: 'Before the race itself, Hamilton had confessed that when he arrived at his McLaren motor home he had been confused because he noted a lot of hostility. Nobody was speaking to him. But that did not impede him later when he showed impeccable form and a brutal psychological fortitude in winning the race.'

The majority of the Spanish analysis focused on whether Alonso would continue to drive for McLaren after the season, or whether he would leave for BMW Sauber or Renault. *Marca* ran a poll which overwhelmingly found that Alonso should leave. *El Pais*, meanwhile, believed that: 'For the first time Alonso has found the support of a team that has always been hostile towards him. It may not now be necessary for him to depart.'

France's *L'Equipe* theorised that there was much more to Lewis Hamilton than at first was thought: 'Dazzled by the precocious blooming of his protégé – who, it's true, has been genuinely impressive – Ron Dennis didn't pay attention to the omens. He ignored Lewis Hamilton's latent Machiavellianism, his already developed political sense.'

Australia's *The Age* also produced an estimate of the inner power of the younger driver: 'Rookie my foot. If anybody needs a hand held over the closing stages of a season turning increasingly bitter, it is Fernando Alonso, who felt the full force of Hamilton's ambition at the Hungarian Grand Prix. Hamilton drove a battering ram through the pretence that teammates can be friends in a fight for the championship.'

The *Gazzetta dello Sport* of Italy bucked the anti-Hamilton trend: 'One fact is certain. The whole world this weekend is agreed that Alonso is out of line. The ill will towards Hamilton, the refusal to look team owner Ron Dennis in the face, the failure to acknowledge the crew at the finishing line, and that phrase in answer to the question "Will you stay with McLaren?" – "I don't know" are serious hints that there is a crisis developing.'

Ex-driver Patrick Tambay summed up a general opinion, also in *L'Equipe*: 'Hamilton showed his personality, his character and his temperament, which are without doubt those of a future World Champion.'

Someone who had taken the sport's ultimate prize was next to offer an opinion. Former World Champion Alan Jones believed that McLaren supreme Ron Dennis needed to lay down the law to his two drivers if he was to prevent their rivalry hurting the team's World Championship aspirations. He also had some sympathy for the current World

Champion's plight. In an interview with *The Observer*, he proffered: 'If you are operating a multi-million dollar operation and you're going for the World Championship, then if you are the boss you are entitled to call the shots. Ron has got to get his drivers back into some sort of order. You just can't go on for the rest of the season with all this going on. You have these highly talented guys and while they will want to do their own thing and not become puppets, there has to be some sort of arrangement. They have to sit down and establish a game plan. It's like cricket. The captain will instruct his guys to do something for the betterment of that team and for the end result, which is victory. That is not doing anything for the benefit of one individual – it's for the benefit of that team winning.'

Alan realised that Alonso's situation had come as a surprise: 'I think Alonso, quite rightly, thought he was going to McLaren to be the senior partner in the firm. Being a double World Champion he probably thought he should get a bit more attention than he feels he is getting. This young kid has come in and to all intents and purposes blown him away and Alonso doesn't like it. Fair enough. Neither would I.' The Australian provided a further interesting insight: 'The first guy you've got to beat in F1 is your teammate. I'd be applying all sorts of tricks, psychological or otherwise. By doing what he did in the pit lane, Alonso might have taught Hamilton a bit of a lesson. Hamilton needs to remember that he is leading the championship and he might require Alonso's help later on.'

However, former McLaren coordinator Jo Ramirez suggested that Fernando Alonso needed to understand that the team would not favour him over Lewis Hamilton. Ramirez believed that the rivalry was already starting to look like the one between Ayrton Senna and Alain Prost in the late eighties: 'More and more, each race.' After the 1989 season Alain Prost moved to Ferrari following two years as Ayrton Senna's partner, convinced that the Brazilian could not be trusted after breaking a tactical 'no passing' agreement on the opening lap of that year's San Marino Grand Prix.

'What's most difficult for Fernando to understand is that McLaren is not a team like Ferrari, who gives preference to one driver,' the Mexican informed *AS* newspaper. 'Dennis has always wanted equality. There are no team orders and Alonso must understand that. That's why I told him he was to get more involved with the team, win them over. Because when I go to the races I see him in a corner with his father and his friends. He doesn't mix with the rest. I can assure him that no one in the team would allow a driver to get a preference over the other. It has always been like that in McLaren. It's against the rules and it will never happen with Ron Dennis.'

Suddenly, with all this being debated, it was announced by the McLaren PR machine that Lewis and Fernando were planning a sunshine holiday meeting before they prepared for the Turkish Grand Prix on 26 August. Contrary to what had been stated before, Lewis insisted: 'Although we did not speak on Sunday after the Budapest Grand Prix, we have spoken a few times since the weekend and we continue to have a professional working relationship. In fact, Fernando and I plan to meet up over the holiday period.' Lewis also stated that he and Fernando would prefer that aspects of their competitive relationship were not aired in public, but kept within the team.

On his behalf, the team also issued a statement denying the claim that Lewis had used the 'F' word to Ron Dennis over the team radio after the qualifying at the Hungaroring the previous Saturday. Many papers had carried what they were told were details of the exchange. The statement read: 'The team have investigated this claim and reviewed the radio transmissions and we can categorically confirm that the use of the "F" word appears to have been invented and repeated to the media.'

Lewis Hamilton had earned a reputation for being polite, well-mannered and personable, and the false rumours were damaging to his positive image. He reinforced his team's statement: 'As an individual in my first year in Formula One, I have done my utmost to conduct myself in a professional and open manner. Of course I have made mistakes, not least during the last weekend. Those are open to public scrutiny. I have my own regrets and have dealt with matters arising. However, it is disappointing that inflammatory and untrue material is given to the media and published, which may damage reputations. This inflammatory material is then commented on by many others as if it is factual.

Whilst I wouldn't normally communicate through press statements, I felt it important to set this matter straight.'

This was followed by further speculation about the future career directions of the two drivers, with a denial that Fernando Alonso could go anywhere but stories being run about a Ferrari bid for Lewis Hamilton. First, Alonso's manager stamped on a story that the World Champion had been given the green light to leave McLaren at the end of the season. On the Tuesday following Hungary, the *Times* had quoted a source allegedly close to the Woking team saying that Ron Dennis had told the Spaniard that he was free to leave the British team at the end of 2007. In addition, the Spanish top-selling newspaper *Marca* had run a story that Alonso had given McLaren an ultimatum and that he was already seeking an exit to his contract. The publication even stated that Alonso's manager had already met with Renault supreme Flavio Briatore. Then all the Spanish press repeated the *Times*' feature. Into this stepped Luis Garcia Abad, Fernando Alonso's manager, with the statement: 'I talked to Dennis this Tuesday morning and he told me what has been published is not true. His intention is that the contract is fulfilled.' As to an exit by his client, Garcia Abad pointed out that there were not many options if the World Champion wanted to stay at the top of the pile: 'To us, it's not a matter of money. If it were for the money, we would be in another team. We are in McLaren to win races and the third title. That's our goal. At the moment there aren't that many options – just McLaren and Ferrari.'

So while that seemed to calm that issue down, up popped a claim by the *Daily Mirror* that Ferrari had been ordered to make a £17 million swoop for Lewis Hamilton. Apparently, the bosses at the Italian giant saw the young Briton as a natural successor to Michael Schumacher. They believed that Lewis had the talent, work ethic and personality to lead them into a new era. Ferrari wanted to capitalise on the infighting at McLaren to lure its rising star as early as 2008. If it ever came to fruition, the offer would make Lewis a multi-millionaire within one year of entering Formula One and well exceed his deal at McLaren. Ferrari's number one, Kimi Räikkönen, would be the only driver on the grid earning more at a current £22 million per annum.

Advice was quick to flow from ex-McLaren driver John Watson and it sounded balanced and reasonable: 'I am not surprised to hear Ferrari want Lewis. Every team in the pit lane wants Lewis. As a driver he's got everything they want. Together with his proven ability as a winner, he has shown raw nerve and unbelievable confidence.' He then urged caution: 'Lewis has already learned with Alonso that if he were to go to Ferrari it should be as the outright number one. There has been incredible politics at McLaren but the pressures at Ferrari would be unbearable. It would be an opportunity but my advice to Lewis would be to let it pass and stay at McLaren. He could easily be World Champion with them at the end of the season and it would be better to try to resolve the problems he's got than walk away from them.'

Formula One's summer break could not have come at a more timely moment. It would do Lewis good. Nobody in the history of the sport had ever fought such class opposition in their first year. He would have time to relax in St Tropez and plan his campaign for the final six races. While Ron Dennis would need to make maximum use of the weeks not only to oversee further improvements in his cars but to try and stabilise a team problem that was on the edge of control.

Chapter Eleven

LEWIS DEFLATED

Unlike his prodigy, Ron Dennis did not attract the attention of the paparazzi during a short holiday in the Caribbean. Yet he was the focus of advice from many in the sport as were eventually Fernando Alonso and Lewis Hamilton. The thrust being that Dennis must reassert his authority over the two young drivers or risk the title being ambushed by Ferrari.

ITV commentator and former McLaren driver Martin Brundle asserted: 'McLaren's boss must remind the drivers of their contractual position, mediate diplomatically, then stick rigidly to parity for the two drivers. This will probably force the drivers to take their own actions. I suspect contact on the track is not far away.'

Former World Champion Nigel Mansell criticised Ron Dennis and his management for allowing the row between Fernando and Lewis to be made public: 'It's something for the team to deal with. It's not something for the public to be part of. It's no different to what happened years ago but it's publicised more.' Mansell clarified the point: 'I drove with Alain Prost, Nelson Piquet and Keke Rosberg. They were all World Champions and they are not going to be your best mates. I just feel some of the things that are happening and the way things are being managed would have been managed far differently a few years ago and it is a great shame. Too much is said sometimes but that seems to be the way of the world.'

The 1992 champion was also surprised that Formula One's governing body, the FIA, was getting involved in the row between the two drivers: 'The thing I find extraordinary is that the powers that be are intervening. It's between two drivers from the same team and it shouldn't affect anyone else. If they want to cause problems between themselves then it's surely up to them.'

Triple World Champion Niki Lauda turned his guns on Fernando Alonso, telling him to stop complaining and get on with the job of catching his teammate: 'Alonso is using all kinds of excuses. Instead of complaining, moaning and bitching, Alonso needs to concentrate on driving quicker.' The Austrian continued: 'My worry is if he continues to find the reasons somewhere else, and not in his right foot, he will lose out because Hamilton is doing a perfect job – simply concentrating on his driving and he's quick. It's what Alonso should do.' As for the team, Lauda added: 'McLaren has the best set-up with the two most competitive drivers fighting each other like crazy to go quicker. When they drive, all they have to do is push the throttle. All the politics before and after does not really count. There is always mistrust between drivers in the same team but the drivers push each other and they drive quick.'

Britain's 1964 World Champion John Surtees believed that the controversial events of the Hungarian Grand Prix would serve to make Lewis Hamilton more determined than ever to win the title. 'That superb win, coupled with an equally impressive practice and qualifying, was only spoilt by the team momentarily losing control – both in the pits and on the PR front – with the subsequent result being that it appeared as if they had left Lewis hanging out to dry.' John also felt that Fernando Alonso was the one who had acted incorrectly: 'I have always rated him very highly. But what would appear obvious is that he values a position that is akin to a number one, and that his composure is very much disturbed by the threat of another team member outperforming him. Whatever happened before, I was deeply concerned to see the very obvious delaying tactics which took place in the pits. I was concerned not only for Lewis but also for the team and our sport. Also for Alonso as he won his championships on merit. I believe these actions showed weakness rather than strength.'

The former champion found himself in tune with Niki Lauda on aspects of the season ahead: 'With the threat Ferrari will be on some of the circuits to come, a united team effort will be to the benefit of all. From Alonso's perspective I think he has treated Hamilton totally wrongly. With his superb record and ability, it would have been far more effective in countering the Hamilton effect in taking the high ground, complimenting Lewis on what he had done and then proceeded to channel all his energies to demonstrate what he can do on the track.'

So it was interesting that on arrival for the Turkish Grand Prix, Fernando Alonso and Lewis Hamilton remained behind closed doors with the McLaren management as they sought to defuse the tension. This initially involved separate meetings between each driver and the leading figures, led by Ron Dennis, at which the ground rules were re-emphasised. 'We run our team in a certain way and we expect certain behaviour from every member of the team,' stated the team principal. 'The drivers subsequently spoke and reached an understanding between themselves. They're completely communicating and neither has a problem with the other.' It was well established that Ron Dennis tried to obtain the services of the best drivers available and offer them equal equipment and treatment. Occasionally, in the past, his requirement of correct behaviour had failed to prevent a bitter division. He recognised this: 'Sometimes it's difficult to achieve but we think it's the way to run a Grand Prix team and that's the way it's going to stay. The important thing is that everybody recognised what their contribution was to the difficult circumstances we had after Hungary and committed themselves not to allow these things to repeat themselves in the future races. It's a pressure situation and occasionally things are going to spill over. But at the moment we are focused and pointing in one direction. If both drivers are committed to driving in this team in a fair way and committed to doing the best they can, I've achieved my objective.'

Lewis was open about how matters had developed between himself and his teammate in recent times: 'After the last race I called Fernando and I said "Look, we can't go for the next three weeks without talking or just relying on what the media is saying" – that we are at war and people twisting things that he's said and twisting things that I've said. So I told him that we need to meet and discuss the last race and how we can move forward, because at the end of the day we are teammates and we need to get on.' So with Ron Dennis's added insistence they sat down face to face on their own, to break the ice they talked about their holidays. Then they got down to the serious business of admitting their mistakes and trying to convince each other that it would not happen again: 'I put my hands up and apologised for everything that went on at the last race. And he said – "me too" and he also said "I have nothing against you. It may have seemed it was aimed at you but we need to figure out how to move forward." We said we have to keep on pushing for the team and we are going to have a good battle to the end of the season.'

Lewis also seemed to take on board his team principal's view that the problem in Hungary began when the team's meticulous plans were not followed: 'We're two different drivers and we have to have two different strategies the majority of the time. That's not to favour one driver more than the other but to defend us from the other guys and to get the best results for the team. What I have to do is do my job and obey the team and not make that mistake again. Ron, Fernando and myself had a lot of time to think about what happened and we don't want to go there again. We've settled our differences and we know where we stand. I've learned from some of my mistakes in the last race, and the same for them.'

All these revelations were part of a concerted strategy of briefings by McLaren to attempt to convince everybody that the rift was now healed. However, to insiders it would be what happened on track in the heat of battle that would be indicative in the final analysis. There was to be a sting in the tail anyway, for Fernando Alonso immediately revealed another issue with the McLaren team: 'What I think sometimes and what I have said is I gave a lot to the team when I arrived in December. I remember the car I drove and the results they had in 2006 and how I brought to the team half a second, six-tenths, whatever, and I don't see anything given me back.'

While souls were bared, Lewis was also keen to express his annoyance at the tabloid coverage he was receiving: 'Every time I go to London, cameras appear from God knows where. I'm definitely contemplating living outside the UK. I've always dreamt of living in London but it's becoming more and more difficult. Pressure on the track doesn't get to me, I'm able to manage it, but in your personal life it affects you.' He continued: 'I can see from the experience of Fernando what can happen. He's so big in

Spain, he can't stay there because he can't go anywhere and live a normal life. I thought that wouldn't be the case in the UK.'

Lewis was especially put out at shots of him on a yacht on the Cote d'Azur with one of the daughters of Mansour Ojjeh, the boss of TAG-Heuer watches and a McLaren shareholder. The press accused him of cheating on Jodia Ma, his steady girlfriend: 'I was supposed to go away with my friends and have a lads' holiday but I thought that was a bad idea at the mid-point of the season because I'm lead-ing the championship and I needed to relax, recover and do some training. I was invited on the boat – there were thirteen of us, including the three Ojjeh daughters who all had their boyfriends there. We had a fantastic time and in the second week I got back into my training. But now I am supposed to be dating one of the Ojjehs, which is completely untrue. She has a boyfriend and we're just great friends. My whole holiday was in the papers. I was trying to relax, but I couldn't swim because the cameras were waiting to get 10,000 Euros for the pictures.' He then elaborated on his problems in London: 'Then I went to the cinema the other day with my best friend and his fiancée and my friend Mohammed. The papers said one of them is my bodyguard and I'm seeing this girl and cheating on someone else. It's not me, you know? I'm not a playboy. If I was then fair play, write stuff. If I can't live a normal life and enjoy my life without being spread across the tabloids – we'll just have to wait and see. It's down to the media really.'

However, with six races to go there was only one perspective now: 'I've recharged my batteries. I have a great car and a great team, and there's no doubt I have a great opportunity. Provided I don't make any mistakes and the team don't make any mistakes, there's no reason why I can't win the championship.'

Lewis was certainly positive about the circuit: 'I have great memories of the Istanbul Park. Last year this was a defining race in the GP2 Championship for me and I am really looking forward to getting out there with the MP4-22. It is an amazing track to drive, with so many challenges and overtaking is possible. The circuit is pretty wide, which always helps when you are trying to pass. Having dropped back to the back of the field after spinning on the second lap last year, I spent the race working my way back up to second. It felt like a win and it would be great to get on the top step this year. It is a very physically demanding circuit, all the fast corners, such as turn eight which is awesome and flat out, and the heat places a big demand on the drivers.'

A distinctive point about the Istanbul Park was the fact that it was one of just two circuits on the championship schedule raced in an anticlockwise direction, the other being Interlagos, Brazil. This imposed extra strain on the drivers' neck muscles, which were usually built up to cope with G-forces pulling in the opposite direction.

It was therefore pertinent that Lewis also emphasised that he felt fitter and more focused than ever for the remaining races of the year. So it proved as he set the fastest time in the second practice session for the Turkish Grand Prix. Despite losing more than half an hour's track time with a slipping clutch during the morning session, the twenty-two-year-old set a lap of 1:28.469 to beat Kimi Räikkönen's Ferrari by 0.293 seconds with Fernando Alonso sixth. In the morning session Lewis was nearly 0.5 seconds slower than the time Räikkönen set in the morning session – 1:27.988. The younger McLaren driver topped the times almost throughout the afternoon session. He was initially only slightly quicker than Alonso, but a subsequent lap put him 0.478 seconds ahead of the Spaniard, who did not respond, although he did predict a close fight between the top two teams: 'We are definitely among the strongest here but as expected it will be a tough fight with Kimi and Felipe.'

The reigning champion was confident about his race prospects after finishing second for Renault in the two Turkish Grand Prix staged there so far: 'The track is great fun to drive. Some sections are really on the limit and what you want to race on as a driver. Turn eight in particular. It tends to be very hot at this race and this can have an effect on tyre wear.'

Lewis commented: 'I am happy with the performance so far, especially as the conditions today were not ideal. It is a shame that both sessions were interrupted, but the work we did was productive and we made good progress.' Ralf Schumacher's Toyota was third fastest in a session that was stopped because of a loose drain cover.

Until his final lap in qualifying, Lewis Hamilton had suffered a challenging day. In the morning free practice his car coasted to a halt at the end of the pit lane. He was pushed back to the McLaren garage and after the team discovered a connector had become dislodged, the young Briton was sent back out on the circuit.

Eventually he would line up second between the Ferraris of Felipe Massa, who secured his eighth Formula One pole position on the anniversary of his first, and Kimi Räikkönen. He was only 0.044 seconds away from the Brazilian's best time and that marked a spectacular recovery. His first serious attempt brought a 1:27.931 lap. This was about 0.4 seconds adrift of Massa, Räikkönen and Alonso. They were covered by just 0.054 seconds. Alonso didn't improve subsequently but Lewis found a magnificent 0.6 seconds. The Briton commented: 'I was quite pleased with that. Obviously in practice we had been quick but going into qualifying Q1 and Q2 I didn't really seem to have the pace. I just wasn't really able to put a good lap together. My first timed lap in Q3 was alright, but I was only fourth and not sure I would be able to challenge for pole. On my next run I got a good exit and just kept pushing. I lost a little time at the final corner but was able to string a good lap together.'

While Fernando Alonso cut an unhappy figure, Lewis Hamilton's contrasting relief was displayed in his banter with Felipe Massa, who was emerging as a friend as well as a rival. Both had begun their seasons as the presumed number twos and both had given their respective number ones a real run for their money.

He and his teammate, who lined up fourth, were on the slippery side of the track. So Lewis took himself off to watch the GP2 race: 'I wanted to see how the guys on the dirtier side coped at the start because that's something I'll have to deal with. Conditions looked quite difficult but I'll do the best I can.'

Despite Ferrari's threat, Lewis was upbeat: 'I know we've just had a short break but not everybody has been on holiday and the team has worked incredibly hard to improve the car. It feels better and better by the race. You have to be sensitive to these things as a Grand Prix driver but I can really tell the difference. I think we have a very strong package.'

As for the challenge of a circuit where drivers were exposed to 4.5G lateral loads for several seconds on such as turn eight: 'It feels slightly different from the way I remember it in GP2 when I had no power steering. The steering may be lighter now, but you're going through there much more quickly, so there's a lot more load on the neck. Each time you go in you try to keep it flat but it's not going to happen because the track gets tighter and tighter. It really is a great corner but it will be hard work over fifty-eight laps. I've been training for it, though.'

The race itself produced drama for Lewis. Massa led away from pole position at the start as the Englishman, lacking grip on that slippery side, lost second place to Räikkönen. Alonso, directly behind, fared even worse and dropped down to sixth behind both BMW Saubers. The Spaniard had to follow until they made their first stops. The World Champion stopped only a lap later than Heidfeld but it was enough for the McLaren to leapfrog the BMW. Once Lewis made his stop two laps later, the Englishman was some fourteen seconds ahead of his teammate. While Fernando Alonso was able to hold the gap, he was not able to make a significant move on Lewis Hamilton until a late race incident. With fifteen laps remaining, Lewis suddenly found himself fighting for control of his car when the front-right tyre blew at 190mph: 'I didn't have any warning. I exited the fast left-hander, turn eight. I saw some bits fly off the tyre. As soon as I hit the brakes at turn nine, the tyre exploded. The wheel locked up and the car was moving around, and I was just going straight. I was very, very lucky to get the car stopped and turned.' With over a mile and a half to the pits, he had to wrestle his troubled machine back for the emergency replacement of his tyre which was flapping furiously. He was firmly convinced of one thing: 'I thought I wouldn't get back to the pits. As soon as the tyre went I braked, and nothing was really happening. It looked like I was going through the gravel into the wall. The tyre was getting worse and worse. When I got to turn twelve the car wouldn't turn. I got to the pit lane and nearly went into the wall. It was a real fight and I'm glad that I got it there. The front wing was damaged and I was worried it was going to damage some other bits on the car. I just saw my competitors going past.'

This was primarily a reference to Fernando Alonso. He took third place, with a re-shod Hamilton hanging on for fifth from Heikki Kovalainen of Renault. Ahead, the Ferraris were fighting a private battle. Massa held a margin and looked in complete control until a few laps before his second and final pit stop, when he was held up in traffic and Räikkönen closed right up on his tail. However, the Brazilian kept his concentration and, stopping a lap later than the Finn, held the lead until the end.

Lewis was philosophical afterwards: 'It depends how you look at the glass, half-full or half-empty. I don't count myself lucky. I think I was a bit unlucky that the tyre went. I was the only one with a shredded tyre. It's racing. I'm still confident going into Monza. We're testing there this week and we'll find out how good we are. But there are still five races left and I'm still five points clear. I sort of lost three points. It's unfortunate. I'll figure a way to get them back somewhere else.'

Fernando Alonso commented: 'To be overtaken by two cars and find yourself sixth going into the first corner is not great. You have to wait for the miracle and it only happened with Hamilton. If someone had told me on lap two that I would have been on the podium it would have not been easy to believe. The final result is the best thing of the weekend. I will not remember this Grand Prix all my life but, anyway, it has been quite good.'

Meanwhile, Ron Dennis talked up Lewis Hamilton's competitive performance rather than just analysing a blown tyre. Lewis had kept the Ferraris in sight when his tyre went on lap forty-two. Having pitted a lap later than Massa at the first stops and accordingly taken on more fuel, there was a theory that the McLaren driver would have closed a seven-second deficit after his final pit visit were it not for the puncture. 'It was a failure at the wrong time. We had five laps more fuel than the Ferraris and we think we stood a real chance of catching them in the last stop. Our pace was good.'

The team principal attributed the problem to excessive heat build-up on a day when track temperatures were so high at a circuit that puts heavy loads on the right-front tyre: 'The right-hand shoulders of all the right-hand tyres down the pit lane were getting high temperatures and, unfortunately, we had the failure.'

In the circumstances, he was not unhappy with the result and believed McLaren would be stronger the next time at Monza. 'It's good to get the points for fifth, and of course Fernando did a great job coming third. It makes the points race very interesting. It's a good points outcome – not what we wanted but we were very competitive and this is a circuit we thought we were going to be a bit weak on. But we're going to be strong in Italy.'

Chapter Twelve

The Italian Job

With what he originally thought was an appeal pending on 13 September over allegations that McLaren benefited from technical data belonging to their Ferrari rivals, Ron Dennis stated that his team's achievements in the 2007 Formula One World Championship would be seriously tainted unless the British team were exonerated: 'We are in Formula One to win. But the important thing is not just winning, it is how we win. I do not know what twists and turns are going to take place in the court of appeal. If we do not come out of that court of appeal with an unblemished reputation then the results of this season will be tainted.

'I know the truth and the truth is that McLaren as a company are not involved in this matter. And I just do not want to find through some process that our reputation is damaged. The rumours and spin that I have heard about this matter just leave me amazed.'

Ferrari had complained that they were not given sufficient time to present their evidence at the Motor Sport Council meeting. So one reason the FIA convened a court of appeal to discuss the issue again was to give the

Italian team a greater opportunity to represent their views. 'It will be very important, this hearing of the thirteenth,' pronounced the Ferrari team principal Jean Todt. 'We want the truth to appear. And it will appear. That is something which for Ferrari, for the sport, for me, I want it to appear. And it will appear.'

As the Italian Grand Prix at Monza approached, what had appeared a distant threat of exclusion from both the 2007 and 2008 World Championships suddenly returned after the sport's governing body announced it had received new evidence relating to the spying controversy. The appeal hearing in Paris was scrapped and instead a meeting of the World Council was convened to hear the case again. At the initial hearing in July the World Council had found McLaren to be in breach of the regulations after a 780-page Ferrari dossier was discovered in the possession of Mike Coughlan, their chief designer. McLaren claimed that Coughlan was working alone, a rogue employee serving his own interests, not those of the team. Coughlan was alleged to have received the documents from sacked Ferrari engineer Nigel Stepney. Both were interviewed for technical positions at Honda but were not offered jobs. McLaren claimed that securing a lucrative role at a third team motivated their employee to act as he was alleged to have done.

In a statement McLaren said that they were aware of the decision of the FIA and that they would continue to cooperate with the governing body: 'McLaren Racing has been made aware that new evidence has been presented to the FIA. As a result we have been informed that the Court of Appeal hearing will now comprise a meeting of the WMSC.'

That this was happening was a setback for McLaren, Ron Dennis, Fernando Alonso and Lewis Hamilton. The team principal in particular had argued vehemently that any team run by him would not use information stolen from rivals and none of the data in Coughlan's possession had 'contaminated' McLaren's campaign.

Then it was revealed that the FIA had granted McLaren's drivers amnesty should they supply information relevant to the spying saga – this in response to an allegation that 'one or more' of the team's drivers may have been in possession of material relating to the case. A letter had been despatched by FIA president Max Mosley to all Formula One team principals plus Lewis Hamilton, Fernando Alonso and test driver Pedro de la Rosa. It urged them to come forward with any material to substantiate the claim. If the trio of McLaren drivers volunteered any information then the FIA would not punish them. However, serious consequences were threatened – possibly the withdrawal of their Super Licences that allowed them to race in Formula One – if it was later discovered that they had withheld information.

In his letter to Lewis and his teammates, Max Mosley stated: 'You will appreciate there is a duty on all competitors and Super Licence holders to ensure the fairness and legitimacy of the Formula One World Championship. It is therefore imperative that if you do have any such information, you make it available to us without delay. I can confirm, given the importance of this issue, that any information you may make available in response to this letter will not result in any proceedings against you under the International Sporting Code or the Formula One regulations. However, in the event that it later comes to light that you have withheld any potentially relevant information, serious consequences could follow.'

The letter from Max Mosley to the team principals contained: 'As you will be aware the FIA has recently investigated whether, how and to what extent McLaren was in possession of confidential Ferrari information. The FIA has subsequently been made aware of an allegation that one or more McLaren drivers may be in possession of written evidence relevant to this investigation. In the interests of the sport and the championship, it is important that the FIA, as the regulator, establish unequivocally and rapidly whether or not this allegation has any basis in fact. The FIA therefore formally request that you produce copies of any documents which involve, relate to or were sent by or to any McLaren driver, which may be in your possession or power of procurement and which may be relevant to this case.'

These documents are defined as material 'which make reference to Ferrari, Nigel Stepney or any technical or other information coming from, or connected with, either Ferrari or Mr Stepney.'

Speculation arose that the 'evidence' related to an email exchange between Fernando Alonso and Pedro de la Rosa. When challenged on this, Fernando Alonso retorted: 'I am going to try and win the last five races of the season and of the other themes I am not going to talk about anything because it does not concern me. This is a lie.' The World Champion was also asked if he hoped his team would be sanctioned so freeing him from his contract for next year. He was firm in his response: 'No way. I believe that if they sanction the team they sanction me. I am part of the team and we would share the same problem. We are here to win the world title for drivers and constructors. We are leading the two and there is no person in the team who thinks that they are going to sanction us or something is going to happen.'

The precise content of the emails was not known. However, that they were significant was demonstrated by the reconvening of the World Council which involved flying twenty-six members to Paris from all over the world.

The drivers were prevented by McLaren from answering specific questions about the latest development. This did not, however, stop Lewis Hamilton from standing up for his team's integrity and reflecting the spirit within that team to take on Ferrari in whatever arena. Asked if a possible victory on Italian soil would boost morale, Lewis was in no doubt: 'Definitely, it is the target of the whole team. That is why we have pushed so hard to make sure we come here strong. Beating Ferrari on their home ground would be a huge blow to their whole team. That will make our team extremely happy. For me it would be a great feeling to do that because of what they are putting the team through. I know my team, I know the people here and I think we are being unfairly treated. So to come here and just do the talking on the track, that is what we will try to do. That is the best way to do it. Absolutely the way to do it.'

There was sympathy for the McLaren drivers in particular within the pitlane. Red Bull's Mark Webber commented: 'I think you would definitely go to sleep at night having in the back of your mind that you have enough things in this game that you can't control, let alone having that to bear. As a driver it would be very, very frustrating to have this cloud over you. If you were in these poor guys' shoes, to potentially lose a lot of their results. They know what they have achieved this year, that's still in their guts. But in terms of the results being taken away from them would be very, very tough. It's not a five-minute job what McLaren has done this year. There is a lot of hard work and toil gone into it irrespective of what information they may have had from other sources. They have still done a more consistent job than anyone else in the pitlane this year.' The Australian also added his perspective on the actions of a few individuals and the impact on the sport as a whole: 'Unfortunately there is a lot of off-track stuff in this business that does affect on-track stuff and that is where this line is now going to be drawn – behind them or in front of them and I think obviously for the case to be reheard in front of a few more people in Paris is not in McLaren's favour. It's getting smelly and it's disappointing that potentially two or three guys could screw the whole thing because it is down to those guys with low morals who are not trustworthy and respectful of the guys they have worked with, and they have stuffed the whole thing.'

On the racing circuit Lewis Hamilton remained upbeat about the prospects for the Italian Grand Prix: 'I felt that our test here last week was very good, although it's always exaggerated when you take the downforce off the car because it feels quicker. I really feel that we had taken a big step forward, as big as the one we took prior to Monaco. Though, to be fair, Fernando disagreed and felt it was smaller. But I feel really confident.'

So it proved for both drivers on the opening day of practice at Monza. After some minor problems in the morning session, Fernando Alonso set the pace with an emphatic 0.8-second margin over Lewis. Both had minor offs during the day as they explored the limits in low downforce. The young Briton commented: 'We went through our usual set-up and Bridgestone Potenza tyre comparison work and now have a good understanding of our competitiveness this weekend. The car feels really good to drive round here and we have made some good steps forward today. However, you never know what everyone else is doing, so we will be looking for further improvements before qualifying tomorrow.'

It was to be Fernando Alonso who took pole for the Italian Grand Prix at Monza, edging Lewis Hamilton into second. Alonso clocked a fastest lap of 1:21.997 seconds – just 0.037 seconds ahead of his teammate and rival. Ferrari's Felipe Massa was third, with Nick Heidfeld guiding his BMW Sauber to fourth spot. Ferrari's Kimi Räikkönen finished fifth after escaping unhurt from a 200mph crash in the final practice session.

Lewis commented on his having 'a good battle' with Alonso, but blamed a lack of balance for his loss of pole position: 'My first timed lap wasn't great but I think that last one I edged a little bit more out of the car. I'm not 100 per cent happy with the balance of the car, but nevertheless we are 1-2 which shows how hard we have all been working, especially the guys back at the factory.' Lewis explained that Monza's blend of long straights and high-speed corners means finding a balance is trickier than at other tracks: 'When you come from a track like Turkey, where it is reasonably high downforce, to here where you have very little – when you accelerate the speed is quite a bit different to what you are used to. Going through these corners with hardly any downforce is quite tough. So you are more relying on the mechanical grip and it is very challenging even though it looks quite simple. It is very, very technical. I wouldn't say it is the most physically demanding circuit but mentally you need to make sure you get good exits everywhere so it is very challenging.'

Meanwhile, McLaren CEO Martin Whitmarsh was telling ITV Sport that the dominant qualifying performance was the right way to respond to the continuing 'spygate' revelations that had troubled the title leaders that week: 'It is the right way to answer it. We have got to stay focused – we are here to win races and win the World Championship and we will keep pushing. I think both of the drivers have just done a fantastic job to lift the team and hopefully will do the same tomorrow afternoon.'

They did, but Lewis's World Championship lead was cut to three points as Fernando Alonso won the Italian Grand Prix. The British driver finished second, overtaking Ferrari's Kimi Räikkönen eleven laps from the end after the Finn passed Lewis by doing one pit stop fewer. Räikkönen's teammate, Felipe Massa, was regarded as being out of the battle to overhaul Lewis Hamilton after retiring just nine laps in.

Alonso led from the start and was comfortable throughout. The Spaniard was only a second ahead of his teammate when the Englishman made his first stop for fuel and tyres on lap eighteen. However, Alonso did not stop for a further two laps and was nearly two seconds ahead when he rejoined. He began to edge away for the bulk of the second part of the race, extending his lead by about 0.3 seconds per lap. By the time of their second stops, the World Champion was more than six seconds in the lead and that was that for Lewis. Instead of pursuing the race leader, Lewis had to focus on beating Räikkönen. The Finn's Ferrari ran four laps longer than Alonso before his sole pit stop and he kept close enough to his rivals to pass the Briton while he made his second pit stop on lap forty. The Stevenage flyer then displayed his qualities as a true racer by catching the Italian car and pulling off an audacious move within two laps. Lewis explained: 'I thought he was too far ahead and I knew I had two laps max before I had the best out of the tyres. But I put in two really good laps and I had an opportunity and I really wanted to make sure it stuck.'

Of course Lewis had a call on the whole race: 'I obviously didn't get the best getaway being on the dirty side of the grid and saw Felipe shoot past. I out-braked both of them – Fernando and Felipe – and I was very close to overtaking Fernando as well, but Felipe clipped me and sent me over the second part of the chicane. So I lost that opportunity. Then I had a second opportunity at the restart but Fernando did a great job to make sure he pulled a good enough gap at the last corner and there was nothing I could do about it. I got to the middle stint and flat-spotted my front tyres and I had some vibrations, so I opted to pit even earlier than my pit stop basically because I wasn't sure if that vibration was going to be something like Turkey. So I thought I'd play it safe and bag the points. We came out and I knew that Kimi, knowing that I was pitting earlier, would pass me and the key was just trying to optimise my pit entry, my pit exit and my out and in laps.' Lewis added: 'I also wanted to do it for the team, I knew how hard they had been working and this weekend we got a 1-2 on qualifying and to get it in the race just put the icing on the cake.'

His thoughts now returned to the implications of the FIA hearing in Paris the following Thursday with the potential for McLaren to be removed from this and next year's championship: 'If you sit down and think about it, I could have what I've worked for and what all the team have worked for – we could have it taken away from us. And when you really think about that, you think "Wow" I could be out of a job next weekend and then what happens?'

McLaren had issued a statement suggesting that the Italian authorities had deliberately tried to disrupt their preparations for the race by notifying senior team members before qualifying on Saturday that they were under legal investigation. This tested Lewis's obvious affection for his sport: 'I never actually thought I'd be sitting here saying I hate something about Formula One but the politics and people wanting to be bigger than others is just incredible. I would say to you all that Ron has always been very, very loyal to me. He has given me the opportunity and he has always been such a great man to me. I have never had any reasons to not believe him. He is going through a time right now where I think some people are trying to bring him down and right now the best thing for me is to give him support.'

The following days would prove that the boss would need all the support he could muster.

Chapter Thirteen

Not So Sweet in Belgium

It transpired that McLaren were 'minutes away' from being thrown out of the World Championships of 2007 and 2008 because of the spying issues. The team were fined $100,000 and lost their points in the Constructors' Championship after being found guilty of receiving data from a Ferrari source. Bernie Ecclestone made it plain that: 'It came very close to McLaren being thrown out; it really was a genuine possibility. A few of us battled on and campaigned for the fine instead.' Had the Woking company been thrown out of the championship altogether, it would have meant the end of the drivers' title challenges of both Lewis Hamilton and Fernando Alonso.

The row centred on McLaren being in possession of a confidential technical document of Ferrari's. However, at the hearing the FIA said emails revealed that McLaren test driver Pedro de la Rosa and Fernando Alonso had been aware of the Ferrari data. As was expected, the evidence revolved around logs of calls and SMS messages between McLaren chief designer Mike Coughlan and Ferrari's Nigel Stepney, but in the emails Pedro de la Rosa talked about information coming from Stepney.

On 21 March, de la Rosa wrote an email to Coughlan saying: 'Hi Mike, do you know the red car's weight distribution? It would be important for us to know so that we could try it in the simulator. Thanks in advance, Pedro. P.S. I will be in the simulator tomorrow.' Coughlan replied to that email with a text message containing the details that were required, although the settings were not actually tried out.

On 25 March, de la Rosa then sent an email to Alonso setting out the weight distribution to two decimal places on each of Ferrari's cars for the Australian Grand Prix. Alonso then replied under a section headed 'Ferrari': 'Its weight distribution surprises me, I don't know either if it's 100 per cent reliable, but at least it draws attention.' De la Rosa then replied: 'All the information from Ferrari is very reliable. It comes from Nigel Stepney, their former chief mechanic – I don't know what post he holds now. He's the same person who told us in Australia that Kimi was stopping in lap 18. He's very friendly with Mike Coughlan, our chief designer, and he told him that.'

The evidence then detailed emails from de la Rosa discussing a flexible wing, aero balance, tyre gas, Ferrari's braking system and the team's stopping strategy. It was this 'systematic' contact between Coughlan and Stepney that led the governing body to severely punish the British team.

If FIA president Max Mosley had got his way then Lewis Hamilton and Fernando Alonso would have been thrown out of the Formula One title race. Mosley explained that he was part of a minority on the governing body's World Motor

Sport Council the previous Thursday that wanted a more severe penalty. He also suggested that if either Hamilton or Alonso won the World Championship, a question mark would remain over the title because the team had stolen Ferrari information in their possession.

Of Lewis Hamilton, the FIA figurehead commented: 'I think he will probably feel more comfortable if he wins a subsequent championship without any of these question marks. There was a big debate in the World Council about whether all the points should go – team and drivers. We discussed whether to take the drivers' points from McLaren, but allow the drivers to drive, don't interfere with their Super Licence and so on. The lawyers felt everything should go – drivers' points and all – because they argued, how can you give the World Champion's cup to someone who may have had an unfair advantage over other drivers? They have effectively cheated. But the other side of it was – here is this brilliant World Championship between Hamilton and Alonso. The sporting people were saying: "If you interfere with that, you are spoiling a very good championship. It wasn't the drivers' fault." But there again, it never is. Very often, for example, a car will be disqualified because it is a kilo overweight which will probably make no difference at all, but you have to have this principle. It's the same as anywhere else, if you're outside of the rules, you are not in the game. So there will always be a question mark over it, there has to be, because nobody knows how big an advantage they had from that. But that they had an advantage is almost beyond dispute.'

Lewis Hamilton was to counter that himself or Fernando Alonso would be worthy champions if they took the title in 2007: 'I don't particularly want to say anything to or about Max Mosley but we have worked hard this year and the way I feel, the team have done absolutely nothing wrong. I have taken the opportunity I have been given and just done as good a job as I could with it. I don't see why people will say, if I win it, it is a tainted championship.'

Meanwhile, Renault boss Flavio Briatore was of the opinion that McLaren's punishment was severe: 'I think it's very harsh. What more could they give to McLaren? Taking away from a team all the points gained this season is a big blow. In Formula One a lot of money is spent and McLaren has a lot less at their disposal now. What was decided by the World Council will certainly be a deterrent. The most important thing, however, is that in Paris the truth emerged and a punishment was imposed. There will be a more serene atmosphere in Belgium than at Monza.'

Flavio Briatore had mentioned the financial hit that McLaren had taken but the team could ultimately pay less than the record fine imposed. 'First, effectively, we still have as an offset the revenue from the points earned to date. That will effectively half the size of the cheque we have to sign, if we ultimately accept this fine,' Ron Dennis told a news conference that Thursday. 'But as you can see if you read our accounts, we turn over roughly $450 to $500 million

USD a year, and we are debt free, so obviously we are a very strong company with phenomenal growth.'

A report by Formula Money, which monitors the sport's financial matters, stated the next day that a sum of $31 million was closer to the mark. The team, 23 points clear of Ferrari after the Italian Grand Prix with four races remaining at that stage, could have expected $68.9 million in prize money for winning the championship, according to Formula Money.

The lost revenue would still be a heavy blow to McLaren – who as well as being one of the most successful teams are also one of the wealthiest – but one they could absorb better than most. As Ron Dennis had mentioned, the company was debt free, despite spending a significant sum on a new state-of-the-art factory, with the team principal announcing at the beginning of 2007 that they were financially fitter than at any time in their history. Again, according to Formula Money, McLaren Racing turned over $228.7 million in 2005, making a profit after tax equivalent to £4.9 million.

Whilst Fernando Alonso had elected to travel straight to Spa on the Thursday and stay there, Lewis had gone to Paris for the hearing. He explained his reasons to Steve Rider of ITV Sport: 'For me it was just important I just went there to support the team. These guys, I have been with them since I was thirteen so I feel very much part of the family and the feelings that everyone is feeling in the team I feel exactly the same way. You know it was very, very emotional for the team.' Obviously Lewis had to return to the race circuit but was kept informed: 'I got back here, I think it was a two o'clock meeting with my engineer. We were walking the track and I had a call to say that this is what they have said in the press. So you can imagine my heart just dropped and to see all the work that the team have done, that I have put in this season, it was going to be taken away. Fortunately I didn't have my points taken away from me and I think we were really lucky with that. So I am going to do the best job I can and just keep pushing for the title.'

As for the battle ahead with his own teammate, Lewis was aware of the pressures: 'I've got to just go out and beat him. It sounds easier said than done but in the championship it is easier to chase than to defend. He is defending the World Championship but he is chasing me and for me there is more pressure on my shoulders to keep the spot that I have. I have been leading since the third round and it would be a shame to lose it in the last four races. It should be quite an equal getaway for everyone. It is a tight first corner and then you have a long, long drag down to the next turn, five. So through Eau Rouge there is plenty of room for slipstreaming and overtaking. So going from fourth to first is possible, even though the Ferraris are very quick on the straights. But I always remain optimistic and look forward to the race.'

When the wheels actually turned on track at Spa-Francorchamps on the Friday, it was Fernando Alonso who moved to the top of the times in second practice, in a session dominated by McLaren. The Spaniard's best lap of 1:46.654 was the fastest of the day, and 0.111 seconds quicker than teammate Lewis Hamilton's. Felipe Massa bounced back from a dismal first session to post the third quickest time, nearly three tenths behind Alonso. Teammate Kimi Räikkönen, fastest in the morning, had to settle for fourth place in the afternoon. Lewis commented: 'Today we completed all our work without any problems. I love this circuit, so really enjoyed driving round here and just seeing what the MP4-22 could do. The balance of the car on this technical circuit is good, but I struggled to get a clear lap all session until the very end. That being said I could really feel a definite improvement in our overall performance since we tested here back in July.'

However, it was the Ferrari pair who popped up and locked off the front grid after the Saturday qualifying session. Fernando and Lewis would start Sunday's Grand Prix from the second row on the grid. The Spanish driver, who spun during his first attempt in the middle sector of the track and had only one fast lap in the final part of qualifying, set a time of 1:46.091 and was third fastest. Lewis qualified fourth with 1:46.406. His analysis appeared on the McLaren website: 'It was a decent qualifying for us and I think that we did a good job. The first session wasn't great but I made some improvements to my driving and managed to find the time in the second session. I thought my final lap was really good, with no mistakes. It is always possible to win and I am pretty confident that I have a strong strategy. We knew the Ferraris would be quick and it will be an interesting race.'

At this point, Fernando Alonso stated that he did not think McLaren would help teammate Lewis Hamilton win the World Championship at his expense. Certainly Lewis Hamilton would not want to be given the world title by Ron Dennis, he would want to win it or lose it on the track. Alonso's future at the team was again in doubt after it emerged that he threatened to leak information about the spying scandal to the FIA. The world number one insisted he was happy and believed the team would not deliberately undermine him: 'They always said they would do the best to help both drivers win races and the championship.' Alonso's relationship with Ron Dennis was now severely strained following a major argument on the morning of the Hungarian Grand Prix when Alonso was moved back to sixth on the grid after being found guilty of blocking his teammate in the pits. During the confrontation, the World Champion disclosed he had email evidence relating to the spy scandal that could prove damaging to the team. It was reported that Alonso threatened to use such information unless he was granted number one driver status ahead of Hamilton. Dennis is said to have called his bluff, telling Alonso to go ahead, at which point it is claimed Dennis then phoned Max Mosley himself, effectively handing his team in to the FIA.

Offered the chance to explain the situation further, the team principal replied: 'When I first heard that Fernando had something on his laptop, I told him to disclose it. It would be totally inappropriate to share the conversation with the outside world. Have you ever had an argument with your wife and said things in temper that you deeply regret? That is the benefit I am giving Fernando. He came to me later that day and retracted his comments and apologised. I accepted it when his manager said that he lost his temper. We have moved on. People have got to understand the nature of competitive animals – they know no limit. I am very generous but my objective is to win races. My job is to win the World Championship, not for people to love and hug me. I am not going to say things that are detrimental to this team. I want to protect its integrity.'

Asked about the row after the Saturday qualifying round, Alonso refused to comment in detail, stating: 'Everybody speaks, everybody speculates, and we are here racing. We first talk about racing. If Ron said something it is because he wanted to. If Max said something it is because he wanted to. I am a racing driver and I will answer questions about driving.'

Ron Dennis then refused to be drawn on whether the Spaniard would be at McLaren in 2008: 'We have contracts with our drivers and we have had no dialogue to change that. Don't be hard on me because I honestly don't know. At an appropriate time we will focus on that and find a way forward.' Alonso's manager had already insisted that his client intended to stay at McLaren next season despite the claims of an untenable relationship: 'We have an agreement.

We are not negotiating with anybody and our plan is to continue here.'

Ron Dennis added a further perspective to the current situation and Alonso's earlier positive comments about parity by emphasising that the team was committed to giving equal support to Fernando Alonso and Lewis Hamilton despite the strained situation between himself and the World Champion.

Ron Dennis also later intimated that McLaren might not appeal against the World Council decision, whilst maintaining that the team had done nothing wrong and gained no advantage from any Ferrari technical data: 'Everything the WMSC disclosed is true. It happened, but I don't believe the facts are proportionate with the fine. If we don't appeal, it's because we want closure and I hope other teams will understand that we're swallowing a financial penalty in the interests of the sport. It won't be an admission that we've done anything wrong. The important thing is the company's integrity and the belief that we never competed with another team's intellectual property.' It was obviously Ron's hope that the afternoon's ninety minutes of racing would provide a respite from months of tension.

Not so as Kimi Räikkönen took his third consecutive victory at the Belgian Grand Prix, comfortably moving away from teammate Felipe Massa in a Ferrari one-two. The McLarens were no match for the Ferraris and had to settle for third and fourth, with Fernando Alonso finishing ahead of Lewis Hamilton and narrowing the rookie's grasp on the championship to two points with three rounds remaining. The result also meant that, pending any decision by McLaren to appeal their penalty, Ferrari were the constructors' champion.

Massa briefly challenged his teammate on the outside at the start before settling into second place. Behind them the McLarens were wheel to wheel into La Source with Alonso edging his teammate onto the run-off area before Lewis accelerated back on track, level with the other McLaren driver. They again ran side by side into Eau Rouge, with Alonso holding on around the outside at the first part of the corner before claiming third position as the track turned right. Upfront the Flying Finn dominated the proceedings, establishing a four-second lead over the Brazilian and maintaining it until the flag.

The McLarens ran longer stints but lacked the pace to compete with the leading pair and even fell 20 seconds behind in the middle stint. Lewis Hamilton went four laps further on his second fuel load in a bid to get ahead of Fernando Alonso. Yet the Spaniard found more speed on his fresh tyres than the Briton could muster on a lighter car, so Lewis rejoined six seconds behind him. The rookie pushed hard to close the gap and went off the road briefly at Pouhon. In finishing fourth, the championship leader was now only two points ahead of Alonso, with Räikkönen closing to within 13 points.

Afterwards, Lewis was not initially restrained in his analysis of the race and the tactics of his teammate: 'For the last few years I've been watching Formula One and Fernando is always complaining about other people being unfair. But he pushed me wide quite deliberately. For someone who looks up to someone who is trying to set a status and someone for a youngster to look up to, he's not really standing up to his position.' It was the start that had annoyed the younger driver: 'I out-braked him into turn one. I was on the outside. There was enough room for him to get round. But he really cut across and pushed me wide. It was quite deliberate. I could see it. If I had held my position we would have collided. In fact, I think we did touch. I was just really lucky there was a run-off area so I could take that.' Later, once briefed by a McLaren PR representative, Lewis had amended his tone. He stated: 'It was a racing incident, I guess. I didn't feel it was fair. I felt there was room for all of us, but somehow I ran out of it.' He had lost traction on the dirt but still managed to be alongside Fernando Alonso as he regained the track and they sped down the hill to Eau Rouge: 'The first incident was the difficult one. I'd hoped to come back and get in the slipstream of one of the Ferraris. But at Eau Rouge it was just common sense to ease off a fraction. Fernando had the momentum and was quicker going into it. It would have been stupid of me to keep it flat but I was tempted! That worked in Formula Three in the wet but I'm not sure it would in a Formula One car.'

The British driver did turn his thoughts to his own per-formance too: 'The car wasn't perfect but neither was I. I did the best job I could but I need to improve. What I always find when I'm behind Fernando is that he's very fortunate when he catches a backmarker. He catches him at the right time and just slipstreams past on the straight, whereas I catch them midfield. To be honest, my race was frustrating and quite boring. It was just one of those races you need to bring it home and finish.'

Ron Dennis was more circumspect about the breathtaking racing between his charges: 'It was absolutely fine. They weren't too aggressive and they're racing drivers. That's what they do. No-one would blink if they were opposing teams. They didn't touch each other; it's motor racing, no problem. You get used to it.'

Fernando Alonso also gave his insight: 'At the first corner Felipe locked the front tyre a little bit. I was blocking the inside and I had no space, so I had a bad exit from turn one. I think also Lewis went wide at the exit of turn one, so he took a little bit of advantage running in the tyre marks. So we arrived wheel by wheel into turns three and four but I was lucky to be on the inside and to get the position there. In this situation I was quite confident with my position into that corner. I was not too worried.'

Of the World Championship situation Ron Dennis observed: 'It's that little bit closer for Fernando to Lewis in the World Championship, but we've got a great World Championship and I'm looking forward to the last three races.'

Kimi Räikkönen believed that everything was possible in the remaining races and was not ready to give up on his title hopes: 'We haven't given up and are still in the hunt. We reduced the gap again. We lost a bit in the last race but anything can happen. There are still three races to go, everyone is so close and we will fight hard and sometimes things can go wrong for all of us. We will keep pushing and see what happens. If we do it will be amazing but we will keep going and we don't give up.'

As to the championship leader: 'We still got points, which is the most important thing. It's down to two points now, but it's not over, so we've just got to keep going.'

The defending World Champion had been steadily reeling in Lewis Hamilton. The Spaniard dominated his junior partner at Spa, just as he did at Monza, and on form he would have to be favourite to take the title.

Chapter Fourteen

Crystal Ball

After Lewis's first race in Australia, the McLaren CEO, Martin Whitmarsh, was already predicting that his protégé would become one of the greatest racing drivers in the sport. What of the perspective of others on the Briton's future career and his impact on the sport?

'There is a lot said in F1 about young drivers not being able to cut the mustard. Well, hopefully we have done some good for some other drivers who are good enough to sit in the seat.'
Anthony Hamilton

'He is doing a good job and has obviously done an awful lot better than anybody expected him to. It is nothing to do with the fact of being good for England, he is good for F1. I wish people wouldn't keep on talking about him being coloured and all that. He doesn't need to have the praise because he happens to be coloured. He is just bloody good. He is young, good-looking and talks to people.

'If he continues the way he has then he is going to be a superstar isn't he? Let's hope that's what happens. Commercially he could be as big as anything F1 has ever seen. For sure. Why not? If he is handled properly and he handles himself properly, then there is no limit to what he can do. If you look at him he looks like he has been around for twenty years. He is super confident, says the right things, so it's good.'
Formula One supremo Bernie Ecclestone

'There's a long way to go and I don't want to tempt fate but he's got the team, he's got the car, he's got the sponsors, he's got the support, he's got the momentum.'
Former Formula One World Champion Nigel Mansell

'Lewis has performed staggeringly brilliantly. He is just so complete, confident and enjoying it. He has reached a level where he has time to enjoy it, which is the extraordinary thing. Lewis is incredible, there's no question about that but I don't think Fernando Alonso is going to evaporate.'
Former Formula One World Champion Damon Hill

'He is outstanding. I watched him in Montreal at turn one of the Esses and every lap he was like a Swiss watch. He was perfect, just "drifting" the car. I don't remember seeing anyone "drift" the car as good as that, on every corner, every lap.'
Former Formula One World Champion Emerson Fittipaldi

'I've known him since he was eight when he was kart racing with my son, Jamie. What he has achieved since then has probably surpassed all our expectations, but nonetheless, we always knew he was phenomenal. My son put a bet on him at the start of the season to be World Champion – and he got very good odds!'

David Richards, chairman of ProDrive, who are entering a team for the 2008 F1 season

'It's just a bit of a surprise, there's no question about it. If he was driving a Spyker or a car at the back of the field, he wouldn't have a point to his name. He's not going to take an average car to those results. He's driving for an awesome team, McLaren, but he's delivering. Confidence breeds confidence.

'My teammate David Coulthard has said the press have said how grounded and down to earth he is, but his world will change. It has to. He will have his own private jet in two years because inevitably that will happen, his time will not be his own and things move on. How his career will evolve will be interesting.'

Red Bull driver Mark Webber

'I would advocate Monaco as a place to live, no question about it. It's very easy for commuting, the weather is good and there are a lot of like-minded, sporting people there.'

Allan McNish, former F1 driver

'Lewis is an inspiration for youngsters to get involved. In many ways he is a role model and what he is doing is super for the sport. He is a wake-up call to the government and various agencies about the fact that sport in this country does not revolve solely around things like the Olympics.

'The motorsport industry is one of the biggest we still have in this country – around £4.5 billion. And when you get somebody who really does perform in our sport, then it makes people think.'

John Surtees, the only man in history to have won the World Championship on a motorbike and in a car

'He is doing a very good job in a very, very good car. Everyone can see that. But it's good for Britain. Motor racing is something we have been good at for such a long time. We have good drivers, good teams, good personnel, and we're good at building race cars. It's great to see a fresh face at the top because we'd all had enough of Ferrari and Michael Schumacher's domination.'

Super Aguri driver and fellow Brit Anthony Davidson

'He has been flawless. He hasn't made any mistakes that I can see and I'm someone who admires success. I'm not jealous. If someone is committed, works hard and delivers, then I applaud it. His start has been phenomenal.'

Red Bull driver and fellow Brit David Coulthard

'It must be one heck of a rocket-ship ride at this stage, a lot of blur. Not a lot of focus as to what is going on around him. He must pinch himself from time to time to waken himself up. It took Hamilton six Grands Prix to win. It took me eight races to win one. When I won mine, I was amazed as I always thought the competition was better than me. Hamilton will be surprised he was ahead of Alonso and Räikkönen. He was out-performing fellow Britons Coulthard and Button overnight. That intoxication and euphoria will test him. A sudden surge of awareness, money and fame is a tough thing to handle. You need real values and focus. He stands to make more money than any sports person has ever made. It's an industry bigger than soccer, rugby, cricket and tennis. He could be bigger than Roger Federer and Tiger Woods.

'He's breaking new ground but this is not par for the course. McLaren have had plenty of disappointments in the past and know how quickly the points change on the railway line. Suddenly you can be shooting off in a direction you wish you had never started off on.

'However, Lewis has been well brought along and developed as a young driver and has been successful in every formula he has participated in. He has obviously got an enormous natural ability but for one so young he still has the mental development required. I believe Lewis will create the benchmark for a whole generation of drivers.'
Sir Jackie Stewart, a triple F1 champion

'Hamilton's success is more than a collection of stats. It marks the dawn of a new era in F1, where raw driving talent is turbo-charged by the appliance of science.

'For decades, racing teams have lavished state-of-the art technology on the performance of the car, and then put their trust in a cadre of humans they hope will drive the result to victory. McLaren has changed all that with its training of its 22-year-old wunderkid.

'Hamilton has undergone an unprecedented regime at McLaren's Woking headquarters, masterminded by Dr Kerry Spackman, a New Zealand-born neuroscientist hired by McLaren to turn their exceptionally talented English driver into a race-winning machine.

'A major part of Spackman's approach is the intensive use of computer simulators, which expose Hamilton to every twist, turn and eventuality of a race until dealing with them is utterly instinctive. Nothing very radical there, of course: NASA did precisely the same with its astronauts more than 40 years ago. But Spackman goes much further, applying insights from neuroscience and psychology to uncover the foibles of Hamilton's technique and mindset, and bring them under control. The result is a driver who combines the standard skill set of focus and controlled aggression with relentless consistency.

'Some will lament this clinical approach to a sport dominated by God-given talents like Ayrton Senna and Alain Prost. Too bad: where McLaren has led, the rest have no choice but to follow.'

www.thefirstpost.co.uk

'In the nicest possible way Lewis Hamilton is not normal. We saw one of the most difficult Grand Prix to undertake as a driver in Montreal. When you have four restarts, you have four times the risk of tyres cooling off, of not understanding the circuit conditions, of collecting debris behind the safety car, of picking up dirt in the tyres. All these things have to be dealt with and he never made one error. You can't say that for the rest of the grid.

'All these guys on the Formula One grid have incredible CVs. They have won championships in Karts, Formula Ford, Formula Three, Formula 3000. They can all drive a racing car quickly but they can't all be winners. There are a number of key qualities that Hamilton has that they don't.

'He has this amazing ability to turn pressure into a positive force. He talks a lot about turning negative energy into positive energy. He absorbs pressure like you would not believe.

'Mind management is a critical attribute in modern sport. These days all the top athletes are on to it. Hamilton has incredible mental strength, way beyond his years or his experience in a F1 car.

'In all sports you have naturally gifted athletes and then you have what I call manufactured sportsmen. It is difficult to analyse exactly where he sits because we have not had a situation yet where he has really had to work with the car to improve it. He is in a Grand Prix-winning package from the off. When the car is a bit weaker than the opposition, then I think we will learn more about his style. Then we will see another facet.

'Hamilton has all the skill sets required of a modern driver. He understands everything that is going on in the car. These cars are like spaceships. You have to analyse and process information in a split second.

'As for making the right call under pressure. When all around are making wrong choices, and more experienced drivers at that, Hamilton gets it right every time. He combines an innate feel for the car with incredible spatial awareness and a sharp understanding of the technical aspects.

'The hallmark of greatness is having plenty of spare capacity when you get out of the car. He always appears to have more left in the tank, physically and mentally. Not only has the car been set up to deliver the best result, so has Lewis.

'Hamilton is a brilliant athlete. Fit in body, fit in mind, his fitness is probably far beyond what is required for a F1 driver. As a result his concentration levels never drop off. He is the best prepared rookie in history.

'In conclusion, Hamilton has all the tools and is brilliantly supported by a well-resourced team. He is extracting the maximum from the available resources to get the job done.

'The frightening thought for his rivals is this: Hamilton is going to get stronger and stronger and stronger.'

Former McLaren driver and ITV pundit Mark Blundell in an extract from the Daily Telegraph

'It is not just me that is impressed. He is thrilling the whole world of motor sport. We are excited about him. The guy is doing things that other drivers don't do. He is like me – he is a racer. My career spanned 525 serious races and I can count the number of racers I encountered on one hand.

'There is a difference between being a very good racing driver and being a racer. Michael Schumacher was a racer – when he was young, not the later Michael. I was a racer, my old teammate Tony Brooks was a racer and after that I'm struggling. The great Juan Fangio? I don't know if he was a racer because he was so much better than everybody else when he was in his prime, so it's hard to say.

'But this boy Hamilton has it. Yet, amazingly he does not make mistakes. Schumacher made mistakes. Everyone does, but Lewis, so far, seems not to. He has the World Champion in his team but Alonso makes mistakes too. Hamilton is better than Alonso, no doubt about it.'
Sir Stirling Moss, British racing icon

'Touch wood and I hope I'm right but he could go on to be the greatest of all time. I've not spotted any weaknesses yet. I don't think anybody has and so far this season he's had just about every combination of circumstances.

'McLaren have allegedly spent £5 million speculatively on supporting him through all the categories, so he's had unprecedented support and he's had a major constructor behind him all the way, making sure he had the best of everything – but my God, he's paid them back ten fold already.

'Every nation needs a hero. The enthusiasts have always been there, but he's generating a revival of interest from the public at large.

'What he's done so far in his career is unprecedented and he's only at the beginning. He's got an enormous amount of potential and development left. The possibilities open to him are, and I use this word rarely, awesome.'

Veteran motor sport commentator Murray Walker